# THE 5 PILLARS OF ASTROLOGY

**71 Beginner Techniques & Tips** to **Self-Discovery** and **Transformation.** Know Your Higher Purpose by **Decoding** the **Secrets** of Your **Zodiac**. Predict Your Future With Horoscopes

## MONIQUE WAGNER

# Table of Contents

Introduction .................................................................................9

**Pillar 1: Fundamentals**................................................................ 12

**Chapter 1: The Basics of Astrology** .......................................15

What Is Astrology?.................................................................... 15

The History of Astrology........................................................... 16

Modern vs. Traditional Astrology ............................................18

Vedic vs. Western Astrology..................................................... 21

**Pillar 2: The Zodiac** ....................................................................... 24

**Chapter 2: The Signs and Their Meanings** .........................27

The Difference Between Sun, Moon, and Rising....................28

Aries...........................................................................................30

Taurus ........................................................................................ 31

Gemini........................................................................................ 32

Cancer ................................................................................. 33

Leo ...................................................................................... 34

Virgo ................................................................................... 36

Libra .................................................................................... 37

Scorpio ............................................................................... 38

Sagittarius ......................................................................... 40

Capricorn ........................................................................... 41

Aquarius ............................................................................. 42

Pisces .................................................................................. 44

**Chapter 3: Elements of the Zodiac** ................................... **47**

Origins of the Four Elements ........................................... 47

The Four Elements in Relation to the Zodiac ................. 49

Qualities of the Four Elements ........................................ 50

**Chapter 4: Modalities of the Zodiac** .................................. **53**

Cardinal ............................................................................. 54

Fixed ................................................................................... 54

Mutable .............................................................................. 55

Relationship to the Sun and Moon System .................... 56

**Chapter 5: Polarities of the Zodiac** .................................... **59**

History of Yin-Yang Polarity ............................................. 60

The Negative or Yin Signs ................................................. 60

The Positive or Yang Signs ............................................... 61

The Complementary Signs ................................................ 62

# Pillar 3: The Planets ........................................................ 68

## Chapter 6: Inner Planets ........................................... 73

The Sun.................................................................................74

The Moon..............................................................................74

Mercury................................................................................75

Venus.................................................................................. 76

Mars....................................................................................78

## Chapter 7: Outer Planets .......................................... 81

Jupiter..................................................................................81

Saturn .................................................................................83

Uranus ............................................................................... 84

Neptune...............................................................................86

Pluto .................................................................................. 87

## Chapter 8: Chiron Planet .......................................... 89

What Does Chiron Symbolize?................................................90

The Chiron Cycle...................................................................90

Chiron and the Signs............................................................ 92

## Chapter 9: Retrograde Planets....................................103

How Does Retrograde Happen?............................................ 104

What Does Retrograde Mean? ...............................................105

Which Planets Are in Retrograde?.........................................105

How Retrograde Affects Each Planet .....................................106

# Pillar 4: The Houses ........................................................ 110

## Chapter 10: Individual Houses................................................113

First House ..................................................................... 114

Second House ................................................................ 114

Third House ................................................................... 114

Fourth House ................................................................ 115

Fifth House..................................................................... 115

Sixth House..................................................................... 116

Seventh House................................................................ 116

Eighth House.................................................................. 117

Ninth House.................................................................... 118

Tenth House.................................................................... 118

Eleventh House............................................................... 118

Twelfth House ................................................................ 119

## Chapter 11: House Positions.................................................121

Angular Houses............................................................. 122

Succedent Houses........................................................ 123

Cadent Houses............................................................... 125

# Pillar 5: Birth Charts ..................................................... 126

## Chapter 12: Creating Your Birth Chart............................. 129

Getting Started.............................................................. 129

Online and Expert Birth Charts.................................. 130

Calculating Sun, Moon, and Rising ........................... 131

Calculating Your Planets ................................................. 133

Calculating Your Houses ................................................. 133

Calculating Retrogrades ................................................. 134

**Chapter 13: Reading Birth Charts** ................................ **135**

What Should I Look For in My Birth Chart? ...................... 135

Reading Combinations .................................................... 139

**Conclusion** .................................................................... **141**

**Glossary** ......................................................................... **143**

**References** ...................................................................... **147**

# Introduction

*There are more things in heaven and earth [...] than are dreamt of in*
*your philosophy.*

**–William Shakespeare,** *Hamlet*

Have you ever felt like there was more to life than what you have been taught? Or that there were more forces at play than what you can see in the physical world? Or that maybe your life and feelings were being shaped by things beyond your comprehension? Well, you're not alone. Spiritual thinkers and healers have spent thousands of years studying these forces, coming up with ways of describing their influences on the world. They have identified several such things, many to do with the stars and planets above our heads, that can explain how these forces affect us. This study is called astrology. By learning about astrology and all its branches, we can understand the world more clearly, finally beginning to comprehend all those mysterious influences that lie beneath the surface.

In this book, I will be teaching you about the five main pillars of astrology. These five pillars describe some of the most fundamental forces at play in our universe. You will learn all about how things like the planets, the constellations, and their movements impact your life and the people around you. I will explain important concepts like the zodiac, birth charts, and houses, all of which have a profound impact on you. You will also find 71 techniques, tips, and strategies on how you can decode the secrets of your zodiac. These techniques, tips, and strategies are peppered throughout the entire book. And it's intentionally designed this way to serve as your guide along each step of the process.

Once you really start understanding how these stars work and your relationship with them, you will be able to better understand your life as a whole. It is only by identifying root causes that we can begin to make the journey toward solutions.

I know more than anyone what it's like to feel lost and burned out. I have experienced so many of the hardships that all of us face today—never-ending work hours with seemingly no payoff, a lack of belonging and understanding of the world, and difficulty with relationships. I knew I had to make a change. So, I connected with my Scandinavian roots, tracing my lineage back to a succession of neo-pagan spiritual leaders, and I began to find answers. These answers helped me construct a clearer narrative about my life and stabilized me, allowing me to chart a stronger course toward the future. I have since devoted myself to the study of many different occult and alternative medicine practices from around the world. As an empath, I now want to share those teachings with the rest of the world in the hope that the wisdom I have gained from my journey might help you.

This book is designed for those with little to no background in astrology. It is meant to guide you through those initial learning curves with the goal of eventually making you an expert in the subject! To help ease you into this rich and complex world, I have structured the book around the five pillars of astrology. We will start with the first pillar, which deals with the fundamental aspects of astrology itself. Then, we will move on to the second pillar, which is the zodiac. After that, we will begin our discussion about the planets, which are the third pillar. Subsequently, you will learn all about the fourth pillar, the houses. Then, finally, you will read about the fifth and final pillar: birth charts. Putting together all these pillars of astrology will help you to start making sense of the universe and your place inside it.

# Pillar 1:
# Fundamentals

Before we get into all of the complex aspects of astrology, we should cover the fundamentals. In this pillar, we will look at all the foundational aspects of astrology, learning the history of the practice of astrology and the differences between different practices. By the end of this pillar, you should have a good understanding of the definition and basic practice of astrology.

# Chapter 1:
# The Basics of Astrology

On your astrology journey, you will be learning about many different specifics of the discipline. For now, we need to get the very basics out of the way. We need to define the very fundamental aspects of the discipline and help you understand where it all started. We also need to make some critical distinctions between different sects of astrology that cannot be confused. Let's get started!

## What Is Astrology?

First and foremost, how do we formally define astrology? Well, astrology is the belief that celestial bodies in outer space (planets, moons, stars, etc.) have a definite influence over life on earth. One of the most popular and well-known subsections of this belief is the idea that the position of the stars, moon, and planets at the time of your birth will have an influence over your personality and life outcome. You have probably heard people say they are a "Libra" or a "Sagittarius," or maybe even a "Leo moon" or a "Capricorn rising," for some of the more advanced astrology enthusiasts. These are all categories to do with the position of the celestial bodies at the time of that person's birth. These categories are the signs of the zodiac and correspond to 12 dominant constellations in the night sky, each represented by an animal or a character. Your "sun" sign, or your dominant sign, corresponds to the time of year during which you were born. Astrologers use a combination of the current astrological map (i.e., where the stars, moon, and planets are at that moment) with your birth chart (i.e., where the stars, moon, and planets were at the time of your birth) to calculate certain things about your life. You can ascribe astrology to any aspect of life. If you struggle with relationships, money, self-esteem, your career, family, or any number of things, astrology can help you both make sense of these problems as well as work toward solutions.

## The History of Astrology

Many cultures throughout human history have practiced some form of astrology. For this reason, it is hard to pin down a strict lineage of where it originated. For example, China has had an independent form of astrology unrelated to the "Libra" and "Capricorn" terms above. In the Chinese zodiac, there are 12 signs that all correspond to a different animal, but your sign is based on the year in which you were born, not the month. So, this tradition is a little different from the tradition we are talking about.

The dominant astrological tradition in the West today is based on something developed in Ancient Greece. More specifically, it came about during the Greek Hellenistic period. The Hellenistic period was a great time for Ancient Greece, a time of brilliant innovation and prolific artistry. The beginning of the period was marked by the death of Alexander the Great, whose rapidly grown empire spanned all the way from Greece to China. The aftermath of this period meant that Greece had much more contact with the rest of the world than ever before, especially Asia and the Middle East. As a result, they began expanding their minds with art, philosophy, and literature brought from thousands of miles away. Many new religions and philosophies of life began to emerge in Greece during the Hellenistic period, including astrology. It was especially influenced by Egyptian theology, which drew a strong connection between mankind and the heavens. The constellations, such as Pisces and Cancer, were already Greek inventions based on their existing mythologies. Astrology took this a step further and assigned these constellations to certain times of the year and to the ruling of the world around us. Thus, the origins of modern astrology were born.

From there, astrology as a concept only expanded. Greece was colonized by Rome at the end of the Hellenistic period, but the Romans did not let astrology die out. The Romans were enamored by all things Greek and adopted many of their traditions, particularly religious ones, and astrology was no exception. It reigned powerfully throughout the heyday of Ancient Rome. Due to Greece's and Rome's extensive contact with the Middle East, Hellenistic astrology also became popular there. However, astrology in Europe significantly declined after the introduction of Christianity to the Roman Empire in the 4th century C.E. Astrology contradicted the Christian order of the universe and therefore fell out of fashion in Europe during this period. In the Middle East, though, it was still thriving. In fact, it kept up even after the Islamization of Saudi Arabia and North Africa in the 7th and 8th centuries. But, for a time, it seemed like astrology was never to be practiced in Europe again.

Europe did not see a significant incline in astrological interest until the early Renaissance in the 12th century. Spain and Italy were under significant influence from the still-powerful Islamic Empire, due partially to Mediterranean trade and the colonization of Spain by the Western

Islamic Empire. Through these connections, Europe began to have a renewed interest in the Islamic culture as well as the Ancient Greek and Roman cultures. By the 14th and 15th centuries, the stories of the zodiac were making the rounds all the way up to England. Chaucer, an English poet from the late 14th century, included many Ancient Greek and Roman stories in his famous epic, *The Canterbury Tales*, demonstrating that this history was on the upswing everywhere in Europe.

The next major boom astrology would enjoy would be the rise of neo-paganism and spiritualism in the 19th century, particularly in England and the United States. The Victorians were fascinated by all things ancient and mystical. Famous figures like Harry Houdini exploited this belief in the paranormal with his magic shows while many other similar figures held public séances and fortune tellings. Tarot cards and crystals also began to gain significant interest, showing how much Victorians were willing to adopt metaphysical traditions. This period of neo-paganism formed the basis of our modern practice of astrology today. Things like birth charts were refined and calculated more precisely, and the discipline of astrology turned into a bona fide science. The prevalence of astrology in the West only grew throughout the 20th century, especially during the new age movements of the 1960s and '70s, culminating in the immensely popular and widespread tradition we know today.

## Modern vs. Traditional Astrology

Now, even though there is this clear line from the Hellenistic tradition of astrology to our current practice of it, there are still some important distinctions we should make between them. Making the mistake of conflating these two philosophies might result in you getting mixed readings or even possibly offending someone. You want to make sure that you aren't claiming any tradition as your own when you are really practicing something else. To clarify, almost all Western practices of astrology, including the traditions laid out in this book, are classified as modern astrology. There may be some similarities or overlaps between modern and traditional astrology, but the two are not the same. Traditional astrology is rooted in times and places different from our own, and modern astrology has been adapted to fit the way we currently live our lives. Here, we will explain in more detail the difference between these two versions of astrology.

## Traditional Astrology

Traditional astrology is astrology as it was practiced by the Ancient Greeks, Romans, Muslims, and even South and East Asians. These are all the premodern interpretations of astrology, the foundation on which all astrology is based. Even within this classification of "traditional" astrology, there were many different traditions. This is why it's important not to claim to be practicing traditional astrology: Every practice from this era is slightly different. They have all merged, with varying degrees of importance, to create our current version of astrology, but no one today can claim to be practicing astrology in exactly the same way as the ancients. For one, many astrological traditions would merge with the local religion. Thus, those practicing astrology in Ancient Rome would have had a different spin on the mythology than those practicing in early medieval Egypt given their differing local philosophies and religions. Traditional astrology had not yet been standardized and thus lacked the cohesion we have today. It was a necessary stage in astrology's development and had its own inherent value, but for the purposes of modern astrologers, it is significant only as a stepping stone toward the current version of astrology.

## Modern Astrology

"Modern" can mean anything from the Renaissance to the 21st century, depending on who you ask. For our purposes, "modern astrology" means the practice of astrology as it first appeared in the early 20th century and, more accurately, as it was more refined in the 1960s and '70s. This is the version that almost all Western astrologers practice today and likely the version that you have come in contact with the most throughout your life. Some practical things have influenced the shift in a more concrete way. For one, new planets have been discovered since ancient times (namely, the outer planets Uranus, Neptune, and Pluto) which have changed the calculations. Additionally, increased communication around the world has allowed astrology, along with languages, time zones, and mathematics, to be standardized and streamlined. Now, much larger groups of people can practice the exact same type of astrology at the same time thanks to things like the internet and even mass literacy. But besides these practical changes, there have been ideological changes too.

Modern astrology's defining ideological feature is that it is primarily focused on the individual. Back at the beginning of the chapter, when I gave you a brief overview of what astrology is, I described it as having a bearing on your life and personality. While the Ancient Greeks did discuss astrological signs as they corresponded to behavior, the idea that your personality is fundamentally a certain way because of your astrological sign is primarily a modern idea. Modern astrologers focus on life journeys and personality profiles. They discuss how the planets might have influenced a person since their birth and how they will help guide them through their future relationships. Modern astrologers can help people to navigate their astrological system, leading them to a future where they are working with, not against, their astrological signs. They might also consult on things like a person's compatibility with other signs and thus future successes or failures in relationships with others. It might also help you understand your natural aptitudes and passions, leading you toward a particular career or calling. In short, modern astrology is more about individuals' relationships with the universe at large, helping to explain their own behaviors, motivations, and skills as well as those of the people and world around them.

The reasons behind this ideological shift vary, but there are two main value changes between the ancient world and our world that have influenced it. First of all, individualism is the dominant ideology in modern Western culture, whereas the Ancient Greeks leaned toward collectivism. We are now more interested in the nature of specific individuals as unique beings rather than the nature of humanity as a whole. Astrology that explains humans' collective relationship with the stars does not speak to our cultural values of individual personalities and consciousness. Second of all, modern Western culture values free will over fatalism. The Ancient Greeks were famously fatalistic, believing that human beings' life courses were fixed and could not be changed, even if the individual consciously tried. Plays like Sophocles' *Oedipus Rex* explored this theme, with Oedipus walking directly into his tragic fate in the pursuit of escaping it. Modern Westerners, on the other hand, believe in the idea of shaping our own destinies and being masters of our own fate. Thus, our version of astrology focuses on how an individual can shape their own identity using knowledge of the stars. They are not huge differences, but they can influence a culture's relationship with astrology and spiritual readings.

## Vedic vs. Western Astrology

Another distinction to make within astrology is between Vedic (or South Asian, or Eastern) and Western astrology. This is not a distinction of time, like the above, but a distinction of place. In places like India, astrology is practiced very differently than in the West. We already talked about Chinese astrology and how it differs, but India also has its own version of astrology. Vedic astrology is similar to Western astrology but follows a distinctly different lineage. It is derived from Ancient Indian texts called the *Vedas*. The Vedas are a collection of Sanskrit-language texts that date back thousands of years on the Subcontinent. They form the basis of the Hindu religion as well as many other aspects of Indian culture. It is disputed when the first mention of astrology is made in these texts, but some estimates date it as far back as 12,000 years. It is unclear whether Ancient Greek astrology was originally influenced by Vedic astrology since there was contact between the two and Vedic astrology clearly predates Greek. Some historians might claim that this is true, but it is unknown. Regardless of the relationship, Vedic astrology has some clear similarities to and differences from modern Western astrology.

## The Similarities

Despite their very different origins, the two are actually quite similar. For one, they share a monthly calendar that determines the relative personality of the individual born in that month. These monthly signs are also based on animal characters that have distinct personalities. They even retain some of the same characteristics month to month, meaning that your sign and its attributes might actually be the same in Vedic and Western astrology. Furthermore, Vedic astrology is also focused on individual destiny and relationships. You will find a lot of spiritual and personal guidance within the teachings of Vedic astrology. So, as you can see, there are a lot of parallels between Vedic and Western astrology.

## The Differences

However, there are also some attributes the two don't share. In terms of practical differences, the main one is that the dates don't line up. Even though there are 12 signs per year that tend to match up neatly with the

Western signs, the date ranges for the months that each sign covers are different. While modern astrology goes by the 19th–22nd of the month, Vedic astrology goes by the 12th–15th of the month, so you might actually be a different sign in each of the two calendars. In terms of spiritual or ideological variation, the Vedic texts tend to be more karmically focused. This is because of the Vedas' close relationship with Hinduism, which invented the ideas of reincarnation and karma. So, though both versions of astrology focus on how an individual acts, the Vedas will focus more on how the individual's actions correspond to their karma and reincarnation, whereas Western astrology will focus more on how their actions influence personal happiness and growth. This is not to say, though, that Vedic astrology doesn't provide personal guidance. It still offers insight into things like relationships, personal aptitudes, and other individual-based concerns, just with a slightly different religious spin. And finally, Vedic astrology ranks the types of signs differently, placing the rising sign as the most important, while Western astrology places the sun sign at the apex. Chances are if you ask a Vedic astrologer what their sign is, they will most likely give you their rising sign first, not their sun sign. Therefore, while the two practices are very linked, they are also not identical and have some sharp contrasts.

# Pillar 2:
# The Zodiac

Now that you understand the basics of astrology, as well as the specific type of astrology we are studying in this book, you are ready to look more deeply into the pillars. In the second pillar, we will be talking all about the zodiac. The zodiac is the chart of constellations that correspond to each astrological sign. It is a very complex diagram that charts the movement of the earth, sun, and moon all on the same image. Essentially, it creates a ring around the earth, mapping out the night sky in a 360° view. This sky view is then divided into 12 sections to represent the 12 essential zodiac signs: Capricorn, Aquarius, Pisces, Aries, Taurus, Gemini, Cancer, Leo, Virgo, Libra, Scorpio, and Sagittarius. The zodiac is the mathematical basis for all astrological sign interpretation. The zodiac signs can also be categorized in multiple ways. There are elements, modalities, and polarities of the zodiac that all interact with each sign's original meaning. In this section, comprised of Chapters 2–5, we will examine each aspect, sign, and categorization of the zodiac to pursue its true meanings.

# Chapter 2:
## The Signs and Their Meanings

Every sign on the zodiac has a particular meaning. When people talk about their zodiac signs, they are talking about the archetype that defines who they are. These signs are calculated based on the position of certain celestial bodies in relation to the constellations. The sun sign is determined by the constellation through which the sun passes each month of the year. When the sun is passing through a constellation, that sign is in sun. The same goes for the moon, which is instead on a 28-day cycle with the constellations. Rising signs are determined by what constellation was over the horizon at the time of your birth and is determined by your birth location. In this chapter, we will look at the importance of sun, moon, and rising signs as they determine personality types as well as the specific meanings of each sign when they are in sun, moon, and rising. By the end of this chapter, you should have a solid grip on all three of your signs as well as the ability to see how they interact with each other on your chart.

# The Difference Between Sun, Moon, and Rising

We have already mentioned throughout the last chapter the existence of sun signs, moon signs, and rising signs, but here we will explain in a little more detail what these things actually mean.

## Sun Signs

Sun signs follow the conventional monthly zodiac calendar. In other words, your sun sign depends on the month you were born in. Sun signs are the core of your being, the base personality traits with which you conduct most of your life. As the sun rules the sky, so too does your sun sign rule your life. This is why many people focus on their sun sign as being their "main" astrological sign, calling themselves a "Pisces" or a "Taurus" without mentioning their moon or rising. When it comes to Western astrology, the sun is dominant.

## Moon Signs

Your moon sign, on the other hand, represents your inner self. This is the person you are when you are alone or with only close friends. It is a vulnerable part of yourself, something you might want to hide or even be ashamed of. It is calculated based on what constellation the moon was in during your birth, which corresponds to the day of the month. Because there are 28 days in the moon's cycle, it will rotate to the next zodiac sign roughly every 2.3 days.

## Rising Signs

Finally, rising signs are the constellation that was rising at the time of your birth. Your rising sign represents your public self, the main personality you project into the world. If you notice a trait in someone else that only really comes out when they are in public or trying to impress others, this is their rising sign at work. It might sound like the rising is the most superficial of the signs—and the moon the deepest—but this is not so. In fact, rising characteristics can run very deep. Rather than representing someone's "fake" side, the rising sign represents someone's social side or their relationship with the social world, which is extremely important. When discussing relationships, be they business, platonic, or romantic, astrologers often look very deeply at the rising sign as it can tell us a lot about how we interact with others.

## Combining Them

All three signs are important to understanding a person's astrological profile. Even more significant is how these three signs interact with one another. Everyone will have a unique combination of the three which influences how they present with each of their signs. This is one of the most convincing cases against people who are skeptical of astrology and who argue that it isn't possible that *everyone* born in the same month has the same personality. This is a simplified and erroneous assumption about astrology on the part of the detractors since astrologers know the moon and rising signs play a huge role in a person's disposition both on their own and interacting with their other signs. So, for example, a Gemini sun with a Leo moon will be very different from a Gemini sun with a Cancer moon. Even two Gemini suns with Leo moons might differ because of their rising sign. Even if someone has all three the same, they might have different readings for the planets and houses, which we will explore more in later chapters. For now, we will be focusing on the main 12 astrological signs, looking at how they manifest in all three versions: sun, moon, and rising.

# Aries

(Figure 1, Aries's symbol)

**Animal/Symbol:**
The ram

**Element:**
Fire

**Dates:**
March 21–April 19

**As Sun:**
Aries are known to be an intense sign. Related to the Greek god of war, they are fiercely competitive and passionate individuals who know how to win in a fight but also how to protect those they love. They might be intense, but they are also fiercely loyal. Another interesting quality of Aries is that they are very open to new things, so you will often find that they are more welcoming to new ideas and inventions than the average person.

**As Moon:**
Aries moons will often surprise you with their intensity. Their competitive streak might be something that only comes out in certain contexts, such as while playing a game or even a romantic rivalry. The competitiveness of the Aries moon will be related more to the deeper things in them, such as love, self-esteem, and family. They will also be more willing to quickly accept new things or people on a deeper level.

## As Rising:

Aries risings might seem like Aries suns on steroids. Since their competitive side is brought to the forefront of the social world, they will seem like the stereotypical "frat boy" seeking out any opportunity to prove their worth. Just know that this is how they show a connection. They don't seek to destroy others, merely to connect through competition. They may also be sexually promiscuous.

# Taurus

(Figure 2, Taurus's symbol)

## Animal/Symbol:
The bull

## Element:
Earth

## Dates:
April 20–May 20

## As Sun:

Often known for being a more chilled-out Aries, Tauruses have the fierce loyalty and headstrongness of the Aries but none of the intensity. You will often not see the big personality of the Taurus until they show it to you. They're the kind of person who doesn't get angry... until they do. It's hard to set off their fuse, but once you do, it can be crazy! Tauruses also have a luxurious and sophisticated side. A Taurus's idea of a perfect day would be to visit an art gallery before being pampered at an exotic spa. Mixing this love for the high life with a keen interest in the intellectual world makes Tauruses some of the most complex and intriguing types.

**As Moon:**

Taurus and the moon are perfectly compatible. Taurus's sweetness and emotional intensity are perfect when put in the moon position. Taurus moons are sometimes slow to accept new people in their life, but once they do, they will experience some of the most profound connections possible. Taurus moons particularly shine in one-on-one relationships where they can get to know people at their core.

**As Rising:**

Taurus risings can come off as a little strange. They won't be the life of the party but rather the cool person who sits in the corner while everyone wonders about their mysterious qualities. You might feel drawn to approach a Taurus rising in a social situation as they will exude allure, but they will rarely come to you first.

## Gemini

Ⅱ

(Figure 3, Gemini's symbol)

**Animal/Symbol:**
The twins

**Element:**
Air

**Dates:**
May 21–June 20

**As Sun:**
Geminis often get a bad rap, but they are really one of the most delightful signs out there. Geminis are social butterflies, valuing the building

of relationships within large groups of people. They are amazing communicators which makes them great leaders. However, they do have a tendency to overshare, possibly saying things that can be considered inappropriate or brash. But don't let this put you off—Geminis can be delightfully cheeky in this regard and make excellent comedians.

**As Moon:**
Gemini moons are interesting since Gemini has such a reputation for being social. Depending on the combinations with other signs in sun and rising, a Gemini moon will likely be more reserved but might be something of a covert social butterfly. They might be able to juggle many close relationships at once, something many people struggle to do. A Gemini moon will also have remarkable honesty when it comes to those deep, heart-to-heart conversations.

**As Rising:**
Gemini risings are able to put their outgoingness at the forefront. Their social circles are considerably more widespread than Gemini suns, and they will be able to start parties and relate to anyone they meet. Gemini risings have an amazing ability to find a point of connection with everyone and will certainly make you feel special.

# Cancer

(Figure 4, Cancer's symbol)

**Animal/Symbol:**
The crab

**Element:**
Water

**Dates:**

June 21–July 22

**As Sun:**

Cancers are the most caring and loving of the signs. They are known for being particularly connected with home and hearth. Cancers will be strongly connected to their families, whether their born or found family. They will not only be loyal to these people but prioritize nurturing them as well. Despite being somewhat reserved outwardly, they have a rich inner life and often are quite connected to their dreamer or spiritual sides.

**As Moon:**

With Cancer moons, this rich inner life is dialed up. Those with a Cancer moon will focus mostly on the deep care and inner spirituality of Cancer. They might be poets, driven to investigate the mysteries of life through their bright creativity. These Cancer moons might have a little bit harder of a time outwardly expressing how intensely they care about others, perhaps demonstrating it in more indirect or nonverbal ways.

**As Rising:**

Cancer risings thrive in care positions. They have the ability to extend their familial circle to a wider range of people, allowing them to ascribe the same degrees of importance to more people in their life. Cancer risings make great nurses, childcare workers, and even social workers.

# Leo

(Figure 5, Leo's symbol)

**Animal/Symbol:**

The lion

**Element:**

Fire

**Dates:**

July 23–August 22

**As Sun:**

Leos are the most confident of the signs. They radiate a leader's energy wherever they go. Leos will be able to accomplish their dreams with sheer determination and charm. Sometimes, that makes people feel that Leos are extraordinarily lucky, but it isn't luck—it's their ability to seek out what they want at all costs. But don't let this make you think that Leos are selfish. They can be fierce defenders of their friends and some of the most passionately loving people in the world.

**As Moon:**

Leo moons are strange. They might be able to mask this inner confidence with a more modest place of work or smaller circle of influence, but they will still rule this with the inner charm and confidence. A Leo moon might not seem confident unless they are with their inner circle, where their more primary Leo traits are more apt to appear.

**As Rising:**

Leo risings are sometimes actually less confident than Leo moons. This is because all that charisma they exude is limited to the social world. They might feel like kings or queens with their friends but return home feeling less confident. Leo risings should learn to extend some of that confidence to their inner selves.

# Virgo

(Figure 6, Virgo's symbol)

**Animal/Symbol:**
The maiden

**Element:**
Earth

**Dates:**
August 23–September 22

**As Sun:**
Virgos are sometimes considered the left-brainers of the zodiac. This means that they love all things organization, from spreadsheets to lists to schedules. But Virgos more than love organization, they crave it. An unstructured Virgo is an unhappy Virgo. At their worst, Virgos can be bossy and controlling, but at their best, they can be amazingly conscientious leaders. Put them in the right position, and they will run things as neatly and smoothly as a well-oiled machine.

**As Moon:**
Virgo moons often have their cravings for organization relegated to their personal routines. They might come across as an easygoing person out in public, but they are in desperate need of routine in their personal life. So, while they might be fine going to an unstructured event, they would be devastated if their morning rituals were disturbed. You might meet a Virgo moon thinking they are laid back only to realize that their inner world is tightly regimented. Virgo moons often need help coming out of their shell and allowing themselves or their personal lives to be messy.

**As Rising:**
Rising Virgos will almost always seem like they have it all together. They're the ones immaculately dressed at the party who show up ten minutes early and help everyone clean up at the end. Depending on their sun and moon signs, they might actually have a messier interior life that they mask with extreme organization. Sometimes they need to learn to bring their sharp minds into the more emotional aspects of life.

# Libra

(Figure 7, Libra's symbol)

**Animal/Symbol:**
The scales of justice

**Element:**
Air

**Dates:**
September 23–October 22

**As Sun:**
Libras are sometimes considered the quintessential air signs since their qualities are so identifiably airy. Libras are sometimes considered to be the flakiest of the signs. This is because they tend to be dreamy and indecisive, easily swayed by others' opinions. But look closer and you will realize this is a strength, not a weakness. Their indecisiveness isn't necessarily an inability to commit to opinions but rather an extreme openness and willingness to consider all sides of an issue. For this reason, Libras are amazing mediators, working very well as judges

or marriage counselors. They are able to genuinely understand where everyone is coming from and thus make a decision that is actually more objective and informed than some of the more fierce or emotional signs. However, this flakiness can easily veer into weakness, especially when in the presence of someone very forceful or persuasive. Libras should be careful not to allow more willful signs to take advantage of their easily swayed natures.

**As Moon:**
Libra moons are some of the most romantic people you will ever meet. They prioritize love and relationships in their life, so if you are in a relationship with a Libra, you will always be their number one. However, Libra moons are especially at risk of being taken advantage of in relationships. They might downplay necessary conflicts or avoid confrontation. Libra moons should take some of their mediation abilities and ascribe them to their own lives, helping them to help themselves.

**As Rising:**
Libra risings make amazing leaders. Though they may lack the natural charisma of a Leo or the competitiveness of an Aries, they more than make up for it with their intelligence. Libra risings are deep thinkers and careful considerers. They would do well to apply these innate skills in the world of politics or even art.

## Scorpio

(Figure 8, Scorpio's symbol)

**Animal/Symbol:**
The scorpion

**Element:**

Water

**Dates:**

October 23–November 21

**As Sun:**

Scorpios are some of the most misunderstood signs out there. They can very easily come across as standoffish because they are a very private sign. Scorpios have a very hard time letting people in, especially on a deeper level. They hesitate to share their deepest secrets and often don't let even their close loved ones know their next moves. This might come across as suspicious or paranoid, but it's just their way of guarding themselves. If they are able to fully trust someone, then they will let them in on everything and have a hard time letting that person go if the relationship comes to an end. One of the most intense signs, Scorpios really know how to commit when they decide something is right.

**As Moon:**

Scorpio moons are often even tougher to crack than Scorpio suns. Even though they might have a very outgoing sign in their sun, letting many people in on a superficial level, their Scorpio moon means that breaking through to their deeper layers will be all the more difficult. The Scorpio moon will need a lot of coaxing to allow someone to break through to their inner shell. But again, once you do so, they will be bonded to you for life.

**As Rising:**

Scorpio risings are very interesting since they are known for being deeply reserved. Thus, Scorpio risings might project an air of unattainability when they are really soft and gooey underneath. You might meet a Scorpio rising and assume they are a very private person only to have them spill all their deepest secrets after a few months of friendship—or even a few drinks!

# Sagittarius

(Figure 9, Sagittarius's symbol)

**Animal/Symbol:**
The archer

**Element:**
Fire

**Dates:**
November 22–December 21

**As Sun:**
You will never miss a Sagittarius. No shrinking violets, Sagittariuses have some of the biggest personalities you will encounter. They are all about living life in the moment and seeking out all the amazing thrills and experiences this world has to offer. For this reason, Sagittariuses love things like travel, adventure, and meeting new people. Any chance to learn and explore is never a waste of time in a Sagittarius's book. They are also known for being the life of the party. You can always find a Sagittarius at the center of a table at the pub, telling jokes and making the whole room shake with laughter.

**As Moon:**
Sagittarius moons will often break out these qualities only when they are with their closer circles. They might explore their love of travel and experiences through more subtle means, like enjoying reading interesting books or watching foreign films. A Sagittarius moon with their sun in, say, Virgo might come across as organized at first only to bust out their more passionate and fun-loving side once you get to know them better.

## As Rising:

Sagittarius risings might seem like the life of the party all while housing some mysterious secrets. You might find them looking pensive at the end of the night, retreating back into that more private inner life they have for themselves. They might like traveling or partying with others but enjoy a more stable and calm life when they are by themselves. Often, Sagittarius risings with more emotional moons or suns will need a lot of downtime in between their socializing stints.

# Capricorn

(Figure 10, Capricorn's symbol)

## Animal/Symbol:

The goat

## Element:

Earth

## Dates:

December 22–January 19

## As Sun:

Capricorns are the high achievers of the zodiac. They are similar to Aries and Leo in their thirst for recognition, but the earth in their sign helps them to stay grounded and work toward achievement for their own personal fulfillment, not just fame or glory. In fact, Capricorns can actually be very introverted compared to the more bombastic Aries and Leos. They will hold their noses to the grindstone while they are working on a project and won't remove them until they feel their work is done. They can become workaholics, but they will also always be certain to get amazing results.

## As Moon:

Capricorn moons are more subtle about their ambition than Capricorn suns and risings. They might not be workaholics or out for recognition, but this doesn't mean they don't still strive for achievement. Instead, Capricorn moons' hunger for accomplishment will run deeper. They might find satisfaction in more personal and private projects, such as writing a novel or even learning a hobby or language. As long as they feel that they are accomplishing their goals and moving forward, Capricorn moons are happy people!

## As Rising:

Capricorn risings are stars in the professional sphere. This is the version of Capricorn that is most at risk of becoming a workaholic. They will certainly go far, but they also run the risk of losing the motivation for their high achievement. Unlike the Capricorn moons, who get a lot of personal fulfillment out of their accomplishments, Capricorn risings might start to feel that their achievements are empty if they only do them for the sake of recognition from others. Capricorn risings should emphasize connection with others in their achievements to continue to give them meaning.

# Aquarius

(Figure 11, Aquarius's symbol)

## Animal/Symbol:

The water-bearer

## Element:

Air

**Dates:**

January 20–February 18

**As Sun:**

Aquarians are unconventional and open-minded. They are freethinkers, intending to push boundaries and forge their own unique path through life. They are unburdened by any sense of traditionality and won't think any less of themselves if they don't meet the standard measures of success like marriage or homeownership. Aquarians are less fiercely loyal in relationships and tend to value communities over one-on-one relationships. This means that they can lean toward interesting arrangements like open marriages but are dead serious when it comes to volunteering for good causes. All in all, an Aquarian is a unique and stunning individual you will never forget.

**As Moon:**

Aquarius moons might not wear their unconventionality on their sleeves. Instead, they might emphasize the more publicly acceptable aspects of their personality while keeping the more unorthodox ones quiet. You might find an Aquarius moon very ordinary at first glance only to learn that they have a different kind of lifestyle or don't really care on a deeper level if you think they're weird.

**As Rising:**

Aquarius risings absolutely do wear their unconventionality on their sleeves, sometimes to a fault. They might dress in a very provocative or artsy way, have an interesting job, or talk very openly about taboo subjects in public. If they have very different signs for their sun and moon, you might find that this "wacky" outward appearance does not translate to their inner life, which might be more conventional. An Aquarius rising with a Virgo moon might be unusual on the surface, but hiding inside is a deeply regimented person.

# Pisces

(Figure 12, Pisces's symbol)

**Animal/Symbol:**
The fish

**Element:**
Water

**Dates:**
February 19–March 20

**As Sun:**
Pisces have a reputation for being the "emotional" sign, but this is only partially true. Pisces are very interesting because they are outwardly extremely emotionally intelligent but actually lack a lot of emotional awareness when it comes to themselves. This is not to say that they don't feel deeply. Often, Pisces will find themselves in the throes of an emotional breakdown that they can't explain. One reason they are like this is their extreme empathy. Pisces pick up on and feel the emotions of others very deeply and are also very easily hurt. They have very thin skin, which can either be a weakness (for example, if they are unable to take criticism or have difficulty watching intense films) or a strength (when they are deeply empathetic and passionate about helping others, for instance). For this reason, Pisces actually do better in less emotionally stimulating environments so that they don't become overwhelmed.

**As Moon:**
Pisces moons can be one of the more difficult moons to have on your chart. This is because your emotional intensity runs deep but isn't im-

mediately obvious to people, meaning that others might take liberties or offer criticism that they don't realize the Pisces moon can't handle. Pisces moons need to learn to understand and communicate their emotional sensitivities to others to avoid these kinds of situations.

**As Rising:**

Pisces risings are very interesting since their emotional reactions are more tied to others than ever. You might even say that their emotional selves are rooted in others' emotions. If a Pisces rising lacks a Pisces moon or sun, then they may not have as strong a sensitivity to things like emotional intensity or criticism. Thus, Pisces risings do very well in careers that require a lot of emotional labor, like therapists or even actors. They can engage in emotional work without really risking their inner selves too much.

# Chapter 3:
# Elements of the Zodiac

Throughout the last chapter, we included a heading indicating the "element" of each zodiac sign. There are four elements: fire, earth, water, and air. This is another aspect of the zodiac that runs parallel to the signs. You might have noticed some similarities between some of the signs. If you look closely, some of the signs where you noticed crossover likely had the same element attached to them. This is no accident. The elements each have an important role to play in the system of the zodiac and each has distinctive qualities in and of itself. In this chapter, we will look closely at the four elements and how they create their own subsystem of the 12 zodiac signs.

## Origins of the Four Elements

You might be a little confused if this is the first you are hearing of the four elements. Maybe you're wondering how they correspond to the periodic table of the elements, which you probably learned about in high school chemistry class. The periodic table has more than a hundred of elements like iron, hydrogen, magnesium, and so on, so why does the zodiac only have four? Well, it all originates from the birthplace of astrology itself: Ancient Greece. You can think of these four elements as a kind of ancient version of the periodic table. The paradigm served essentially the same purpose: to explain the forces at play in the world around us.

Because the Ancient Greeks didn't have microscopes with which to observe the minutiae of the natural world, they used their naked senses to discern what elements were controlling the world. They came up with four forces that they believed described the world around them. The first was earth, encompassing everything from dirt to rocks to plants and animals, even humans themselves. The second was water, appearing as seas or rivers or rainstorms. The third was fire, a force of warmth and life but also of destruction. And finally, there was air, representing the space between everything up to the heavens as well as wind and breath.

By categorizing the elements into these four simple forces, the Greeks were able to describe some very fundamental aspects of human life. To this day, you can still categorize many of the periodic table's elements into earthen elements (minerals and rocks), fiery elements (such as gases), aquatic or liquid elements, and those which evaporate into the air. This system of elements was also closely related to the Greek gods, mythology, and of course astrology as well. Today, we observe the element system as a central aspect of both the zodiac and other spiritual practices, such as tarot cards. In tarot, the elements each rule over a suit in the deck, also corresponding to four aspects of life discussed in tarot readings. So, even thousands of years later, the four Greek elements still play an important role in helping us understand the universe.

# The Four Elements in Relation to the Zodiac

When the Greeks developed their system of the four elements, they wove them into many of their spiritual practices. They assigned meanings to these elements, which all related to constellations, planets, and gods. You may have heard of earth goddesses like Demeter or water gods like Poseiden. The idea that the wind, sea, fire, and land were all ruled by fanciful gods was central to Greek theology and helped them make sense of things like extreme weather, plagues, and even personal tragedy. They were also a lens through which people could be viewed, corresponding certain behaviors to "fieriness" or "airiness," which formed the basis of the personality-centric sign system.

The elements relate to the zodiac calendar in a very mathematical way. Because 12 divides neatly by four, you get a clean three signs for each element. The elements also alternate in perfect sequence through the calendar. If you go back and read the last chapter, you will see that the elements play out in a particular pattern. The elements that are mapped onto each zodiac sign relate to the symbol that the sign represents. Some have more obvious connections than others. Pisces, the fish, is a water sign, while Capricorn, the goat, is earth. Some are difficult to connect at first, such as Libra, the scales, being an air sign, or Sagittarius, the archer, being a fire sign. However, if you look at the mythological significance of these constellations, their meanings will line up more thematically with the element in question. By being mapped onto the 12-sign zodiac system, the elements run parallel to the signs, creating another layer of meaning behind them.

# Qualities of the Four Elements

As we mentioned above, each element has its own distinct qualities. You can see how signs of the same element echo one another, suggesting that though they have some different superficial qualities, they share a deeper connection. Some people value their sign's element very highly, proclaiming that they are an "air sign" or an "earth sign" as confidently as they would assert that they were a Taurus or a Scorpio. In this section, we will look at the deeper archetypal meanings behind each element and how they connect the three astrological signs that they rule.

## Air

Presiding over Aquarius, Gemini, and Libra, air signs share a penchant for two essential things: logic and sociability. All three of these signs are unemotional thinkers who have the ability to look past emotions and think rationally. They are also, in a way that might seem contradictory, lovers of communication and socializing. The worst quality of the air signs is their flightiness. They have a tendency to be somewhat flippant or nonchalant about the deeper connections in life. They might end up abandoning relationships without much thought or struggle to stick to their opinions, values, or even personality traits. Air signs are great people to have on your side, though. Immensely intelligent and brave, they will always be interesting. In the Tarot, air signs are represented by the suit of swords, which denotes truth and intellectual pursuits.

## Earth

Considered to be the polar opposite of the air signs, earth is the—you guessed it—down-to-earth element. Virgos, Tauruses, and Capricorns all share earth as their ruler. An earth sign will be a strong force in any situation, although not as an aggressor but rather as a quiet strength that stays true through thick and thin. It takes a lot to sway an earth sign, and they will likely be skeptical of anyone they perceive as fake or manipulative. Because they are so grounded in reality, earth signs are very hard to fool and might even bring out an authenticity you didn't know you had. That being said, earth signs can lean toward the boring side. They are quick to judge and therefore quick to dismiss, often being the last to adopt a new idea or social movement. Despite this extreme caution, you will never find someone as steadfast as an earth sign. In the Tarot, earth is represented by the pentacle suit, which focuses on money, practical concerns, and material prosperity.

## Water

Connected to Cancer, Scorpio, and Pisces, water signs are considered to be the emotional signs. Water signs feel emotions very deeply and are also very caring toward others. We can see in each of these three signs how this manifests slightly differently. For Cancers, it's all about taking care of those they love and pursuing happiness through nurturing. For Scorpios, it's about shielding themselves from the extremity of the emotions they keep so deep inside. And for Pisces, it's about feeling as deeply and intensely as possible at every opportunity. As is probably obvious, water signs can be the most sensitive of the signs, which can be a good and a bad thing. At their worst, water signs can be needy and easily hurt, requiring others to walk on eggshells around them. At their best, water signs turn their emotions outward and use that intelligence to heal those around them. If you're in need of a deeply loving partner, look no further than a water sign. In the Tarot, water corresponds to the cup suit, which predicts events relating to family and relationships.

## Fire

Finally, we get to the most intense of the elements. Fire rules Leo, Aries, and Sagittarius. It is obviously the most intense and passionate of the elements, bearing striking similarities to the physical form of fire.

Besides intensity and passion, what fire signs really share is confidence and charisma. As with all the other elements, there are good and bad sides to this. At their worst, fire signs can be vain, a love of themselves turning into disinterest in others. A fire sign who has given in to their worst qualities might come across as conceited or even narcissistic. At their best, though, fire signs can be the life of the party, amazing leaders, and brilliant artists. Many famous actors and rock stars are fire signs, letting their confidence propel them to greatness without letting it get to their heads. In Tarot, fire corresponds to the wand suit and deals with creative inspiration and execution.

# Chapter 4:
# Modalities of the Zodiac

B esides the elements, there are other ways of dividing up the zodiac signs. One of these is called modalities, and it represents the way that the signs pursue activities. While the elements more have to do with the core values and personality traits of the signs, the modalities are more connected to behavior and choices. Like the elements, the modalities map very neatly onto the 12 zodiac signs. However, instead of four groups of three, the modalities have three groups of four. The three modalities are cardinal signs, fixed signs, and mutable signs. Each modality has four signs it rules over. As with the elements, signs that share the same modality will all have certain similar characteristics, though they are different from the shared qualities of the elements. Because of the perfect mathematics of the zodiac, each modality will have one sign that represents each element, allowing us to see how the elements can be broken up and recategorized along a different framework. In this chapter, we will explore the three modalities and their relationships to the zodiac signs they rule over.

# Cardinal

The cardinal signs are Aries, Cancer, Libra, and Capricorn. The quality that distinguishes cardinal signs most of all is their energy. Cardinal signs are considered the go-getters of the zodiac. If you look back at some of their descriptions, you will see that a forward drive, whether that's in pursuit of competition, emotional depth, truth, or professional success, cardinal signs are always moving forward toward their goals. Cardinals are also known for being "idea" people, always innovating and thinking of new ways to improve the world. They are visionaries, living off inspiration and drive.

What's interesting about these different methods of categorizing is that they bring out different aspects of each sign and demonstrate how intersecting value systems can highlight one trait or another. For example, Aries is both a fire sign and a cardinal sign. This means that its fellow fire sign, Leo, might share the core trait of confidence but does not share the action trait of constant pursuit. Thus, these fire signs are connected in one regard but not in another, showing how multifaceted each sign truly is. The fact that Aries, Cancer, Libra, and Capricorn are all fairly superficially different also demonstrates that modalities are not as close to the surface as the elements. While you might be able to spot an air sign from a mile away, it might take you a little bit more time to spot someone's modality in the same way. Modalities really demonstrate how someone's behavior can cut through personality lines and form bonds between unlikely types.

# Fixed

In the fixed category, you will find Taurus, Leo, Scorpio, and Aquarius. Fixed signs are the doers, the practical implementers that take the spearheading cardinal ideas and turn them into reality. The defining characteristic of fixed signs is perseverance. While cardinal signs might struggle with losing interest or burnout because of their intense bursts of energy, fixed signs are able to keep going even when the road ahead seems tough or boring. Finding joy in the accomplishment of each step is how fixed signs keep their interest afloat. You won't find a fixed sign giving up easily. In fact, it takes a lot for them to genuinely abandon a task. The other secret weapon that fixed signs have in their back pockets is inherent confidence. Where cardinal signs gain confidence from their amazing ideas, fixed signs gain confidence from proof of their undeniable success. They are able to point to the things they have accomplished and say, "I know I can do that again." Finally, fixed signs also share remarkable patience. They are not swayed when a project takes longer than they think it will. In fact, they are sometimes encouraged by this because they adore the methodology so much.

# Mutable

Gemini, Virgo, Sagittarius, and Pisces are the lineup for the mutable signs. Mutable signs, as their name suggests, are looser than the other signs and able to adapt to any situation very easily. They are not usually the signs that spearhead huge movements, nor the ones that slog through the long process to get them done. They are, however, the ones who see to it that the finer details always fall into place. These are the very malleable signs, the ones that will go with whatever the majority wants. However, this doesn't mean that mutable signs are mindless sheep. Mutable signs are actually very intelligent, it's just that they don't tend toward strong convictions or leadership. They prefer to make use of what they have, putting their exceptional resourcefulness to good use. If the mutable signs had a motto, it would be "You get what you get, and you don't get upset," or rather, "You get what you get, and you do something amazing with it!"

# Relationship to the Sun and Moon System

So, how does the modality system relate to the concepts we talked about in Chapter 2 regarding the specific signs and their qualities? More precisely, how do these signs and qualities relate to your sun, moon, and rising positions? You may have been asking yourself, "What does it mean if I have a mutable rising? Or a cardinal moon? What if all my signs are in the same modality? What if I have all three in my chart?" These are all amazing questions that have very definitive answers in astrological philosophy. In the earlier chapters, I said that the modalities represented your behavior or choices more so than your personality, but even this distinction can be broken down further. In fact, the modalities have very clear purposes when put into the context of sun, moon, and rising, representing three very different sides of this behavioral approach.

## Sun Modalities

The sun sign, as we have already discussed, represents the core of your identity. Thus, the way your sun sign affects your modality has to do very clearly with your general behavioral patterns. This is the overarching way that you behave in most contexts, particularly those that are very neutral. Your sun modality is fundamental enough that it will meaningfully affect the rest of the modalities, representing a sort of base framework for the moon and rising modality.

## Moon Modalities

The moon in the general zodiac represents your inner self, but its meaning changes slightly when brought into the world of the modalities. Instead of your general inner self, the moon modality represents your emotional life and your relationships with others. When we look at the modalities from this perspective, their meaning changes a little bit. Cardinal moons are usually the initiators in relationships. They are usually the first to ask others out, plan dates with their significant others, and come out with big gestures for their friends or partners. In other words, cardinal moons are amazing at reaching out and forging connections with new people and reconnecting with those already in their life. Fixed moons are amazing at emotional maintenance. Once you have established a relationship with a fixed moon, you know they will never neglect that relationship. They keep a close watch on the people in their lives. When it comes to mutable moons, they are usually the more accommodating members of a relationship. They want to keep their partner happy at all costs and will ensure that nothing happens to make the other upset. This might seem like walking on eggshells, but it is actually a careful kind of consideration. So, we can see how the moon position will affect how your modality is read.

# Chapter 5:
## Polarities of the Zodiac

The third way in which the signs of the zodiac are sectioned off is through something called polarities. The term "polarities" usually refers to a binary or spectrum system. In the case of the zodiac, polarity refers to two groups of signs. In Chapters 3 and 4, we looked at different groupings of the zodiac signs, the first being four groups of three and the second being three groups of four. Now, with the polarities, we will be looking at two groups of six as well as six groups of two, classifying the zodiac signs into two categories as well as into pairs of opposites that complement and challenge each other. The polarities of the zodiac are based on the system of yin and yang, or positive and negative energies. Don't be intimidated by what seems like a value judgment. Even if your sign is "negative," it doesn't necessarily mean that you are a negative person. These things are simply archetypes and complex categorizations we can use to better understand the zodiac. In this chapter, we will look at the relationship between yin and yang and the zodiac.

# History of Yin-Yang Polarity

As you might already know, the concepts of yin and yang are an ancient Chinese idea born in the 3rd century B.C.E. You are probably most familiar with it through its iconic symbol of the black and white sections making up a single circle. Each section has a smaller section with its opposing color inside, illustrating some of the complexity of yin and yang, suggesting that each has a part of the other inside of them. In Chinese mythology, yin and yang are the origin forces of the universe. Back before all the complex matter we have today, there were only two forces: chaos and control, masculine and feminine, dark and light. The world existed only in opposite but complementary forces. As the universe grew in complexity, the base of these opposite forces remained. Today, according to this philosophy, everything can be categorized into yin and yang forces, allowing us to see and interpret the world as being a part of these base concepts from the beginning of time. In relation to the zodiac, both the Chinese and Western zodiacs employ polarity as a method of grouping the signs as archetypes. Not only this, but they have also paired the opposing signs with specific ones that are considered to be connected. Using the concept of yin and yang, we can observe how opposing forces interact with and mold each other, whether in the zodiac or outside of it.

# The Negative or Yin Signs

First, we are going to look at the way polarity appears on the yin side of the zodiac. This half of the system is ruled by many concepts that have corresponding yang opposites. As an overview, yin is the feminine side, represented by things like the moon, darkness, passivity, water, transformation, and the spirit world. Yin is thus shrouded in mystery, embodying the dark and unseen forces that underpin all life on earth.

It is not a force of evil. In fact, yin is a force that digs deeper into the inner meaning of things, weighing people down with the knowledge of their spiritual truths. If you are looking for guidance at the deepest layer of yourself, you should look toward yin forces. Yin does have a bad side though. It can become misguided to dwell only on these mysterious philosophical and spiritual forces, losing track of your real life. When dwelling in yin, remember not to become stuck in the spirit world, and make sure you have that little bit of yang left to guide you out when you need it.

The yin zodiac signs are Cancer, Scorpio, Pisces, Capricorn, Taurus, and Virgo. The first thing you will probably notice about this list is that these are all water and earth signs. Water and earth are the yin elements because they are the "heavier" elements. Water and earth are both bound to the core of the planet, never flying up to the heavens. They are also life-sustaining elements, providing hydration and nutrients for life on earth. Finally, earth and water are also where mysterious forces lie. Deep oceans and thick forests house mysterious creatures. Most mythologies include these kinds of settings as places of dark mystery but also deep spirituality. If you are a yin sign, you probably feel a strong connection to the spirit world, to the higher questions in life, and to your deepest feelings. It is an essential element of anyone's chart, helping them through life's metaphysical side.

## The Positive or Yang Signs

On the other side of the spectrum, we have yang. Yang represents all the things that yin lacks. As the masculine pole, yang presides over forces like light, the sun, youth, activity, and mountains. Yang is the doing pole; it is all about movement and taking action in the real world. You will notice that rationality and irrationality do not appear in this binary.

This is because both sides have elements of rationality and irrationality to them. While yang is certainly more functional in the real world than yin, it also is an important force in creativity and imagination. Rather than being grounded by yin's strong earthen energy, yang is able to fly up and dream of new possibilities for change. Progress and innovation are yang's bread and butter.

The rest of the signs on the zodiac are the yang signs: Aries, Leo, Sagittarius, Libra, Aquarius, and Gemini. To complement the yin signs, these are all air and fire signs. Air and fire are both free elements, flowing in the wind or crackling toward the sky. Unlike earth and water, which are weighed down, air and fire are light and, therefore, unburdened. If you are a yang sign, you are probably a very energetic person who doesn't bother too much with the "why" of it all—you're just interested in the "how." The negative side of yang is forgetting to investigate those deeper questions in life in order to give all that activity more profound meaning. Make sure that you dip your toe in the waters of yin once in a while to make sure you really understand the purpose behind your life and actions.

## The Complementary Signs

As I said at the beginning of the chapter, the other aspect of the yin-yang categorization of the zodiac is complementary signs. This polarity works somewhat separately from the yin-yang dichotomy since all the opposites are actually within their respective yin-yang categories. The fact that the complementary signs can even exist within an overarching category shows the diversity of yin and yang as well as the multifaceted nature of the zodiac signs. This complementary system does not necessarily have to do with compatibility. There are many factors that go into whether two sides are compatible with each other or not. However, these two signs will certainly bring about something in each other. Because of their opposing nature, they will often ignite a deep connection of opposites but also possibly a clashing of philosophies and values. It's the kind of relationship which might begin with contention and seeming incompatibility but will ultimately end with much learning on both sides. In this section, we will look at each pair of complementary signs to examine their relationship with one another.

## Virgo and Pisces

Given the extremely logical nature of earthly Virgo and the emotional nature of watery Pisces, these signs seem diametrically opposed. On the surface, it seems as if they would have absolutely nothing to say to one another. However, since these are both extreme signs, each extreme can actually lend some much-needed balance to the pair. This is not a relationship born out of extreme love and passion but rather mutual respect. For this reason, Virgo and Pisces make a good pair in many different contexts, usually consisting of institutions. As work colleagues, friends, and even artistic collaborators, Virgo and Pisces are able to bring their polarized qualities together to make something truly magical. In terms of marriage, you will find a very steady relationship between Virgo and Pisces. They might not have the passionate ups and downs that can make a marriage exciting, but they will have the commitment and drive to make it work no matter what. As we can see, the balance of Virgo and Pisces makes for a very well-rounded pair.

## Leo and Aquarius

Moving on to a fire and an air sign, Leo and Aquarius also have some very contradictory traits. For one, Leos feel the need to be well-liked while Aquarians very much march to the beat of their own drums. Thus, it can be easy for Leos to look at Aquarians as weird or even deviant, while Aquarians might tend to think of Leos as show-offs or conformists. Their extreme difference in social values can very easily lead to some strong clashes. However, if Leos and Aquarians are able to look deeper into themselves and each other to see the hidden qualities underneath, they will be able to find some common ground. They are both fiercely loyal signs who also share a strong ambition. If they are able to fuse these things, they will become full of dynamism. What results is a passionate relationship that might not have the staying power of Virgo and Pisces, but which more than makes up for it with intensity.

## Cancer and Capricorn

One of the most compatible pairs in this group of signs, Cancer and Capricorn have sometimes been called perfect lovers. The reason for this compatibility comes from an ideal combination of perfect values and differing personalities. Where Capricorns are extremely forceful, Cancers are easygoing. Where Cancers are perceptive and nurturing, Capricorns are iron-skinned and strong. These dichotomies fit together like puzzle pieces, feeding off one another in a harmony of reciprocal care. They seem to have every quality that the other lacks, making any relationship between them very fruitful. The main danger between these two is that Capricorn's coldness can harm Cancer's soft interior. Cancers might also struggle to get Capricorns to come out of their relatively tough emotional shell, possibly causing friction over a lack of open communication between the two. But as long as they both establish proper boundaries and know what each others' touchy points are, especially Cancer's, then they will get along famously.

## Gemini and Sagittarius

Another fire and air pair, Gemini will fan Sagittarius's flames beautifully. These signs are actually fairly similar, despite being opposite on the zodiac wheel. Because they are both mutable, they are incredibly easygoing and work hard to accommodate the other when needed. Thus, you will find few conflicts between them for a complementary pair. They will be a very passionate couple who seem attached at the hip, both best friends and lovers at the same time. This can be a blessing and a curse. On one hand, they will have a deeply engaging and fulfilling relationship that can push them both past the boundaries of what they thought was possible. Yet, at the same time, it can also cause them to lose track of the real world, preferring to stay in their own little invented world together. The notable lack of earth in this pairing means that flying off into the sky is always a possibility. If one or both have some strong earth elsewhere in their chart, especially in their moon, then they will be able to keep their adventurous escapades grounded in reality. All in all, these signs have amazing compatibility.

## Taurus and Scorpio

Taurus and Scorpio are one of the most spark-inducing compatibilities out there, and also one of the most volatile. When it comes to these two, it's really all about cycles of intense attraction and repulsion, sometimes at the same time! When they meet, they will instantly notice each other, establishing an electricity that will define the rest of their relationship. Unfortunately, this extremely intense relationship often struggles to get past the honeymoon phase. Contention and unrest await Tauruses and Scorpios when the initial excitement has worn off. They are often found fighting intensely very shortly into a relationship which, if the commitment is missing, might cause them to give up on each other altogether. If they intend to make their relationship last, they will have to learn to work through the disagreements they will inevitably have.

## Aries and Libra

Two passionate signs at their core, Aries and Libra can be a great match. They will have high compatibility in the passion department, but they will also have enough levelheadedness to get through the messier side of the relationship. The main issue Aries and Libras might run into is an incompatibility of wills. Unlike a lot of the other sign pairs on this list, Aries and Libra have very mismatched wills as Aries is very forceful and Libra is comparatively meek. They might find themselves falling into an uneven power dynamic, with Aries always taking the lead and Libra always following. When it comes to trivial things like taste in music, this needn't be an issue, but when it comes to bigger things, Libra needs to learn to use their voice in the relationship, making sure that they don't get walked all over.

# Pillar 3:
# The Planets

So far, we have talked exclusively about the sun, moon, and constellations. These are some of the more important parts of the zodiac system, but they are only pieces of the whole. Even though the zodiac might already seem very complex, with many different forms and categories of signs, it is still more complex. Astrologers are also very interested in the planets and how they interact with the sky and subsequently influence human behavior. The word "planet" is actually derived from the Greek word meaning "wanderer." This was because planets appeared like stars but behaved differently from them. To the Ancient Greeks, it seemed like the night sky consisted of five (at the time there were only five observable planets) stars which did not stick to the constellation forms at all but rather appeared in a different place in the sky every night.

Thus, the Greeks attached special importance to these celestial bodies, which seemed to have minds and personalities of their own. In fact, they even named these planets after their gods, thereby attaching all the mythology and meaning of that particular god to the planet. Today, we use the Romanization of the planet names but retain the meanings. Mercury, the closest planet to the sun, is based on the Greek god Hermes, the messenger of the gods who can run very fast, just like Mercury's quick orbit. Venus, Mercury's neighbor, is named for Aphrodite, the goddess of love. Mars, also known as Aries, is the god of war, matching the bloodred intensity of Mars's surface. Jupiter, the Roman version of Zeus, is so named for being the biggest of the planets and thus the ruler. And finally, the furthest observable planet at the time was named Saturn, called Cronos in Greek, who is the oldest and father of all the gods, famous for devouring his children. These five planets make up the basis of Greek planetary astrology.

The zodiac, however, acknowledges ten planets. So, where do the other five come from? Well, three more came during the Renaissance when, thanks to inventors and astronomers like Galileo, the first astronomical telescopes were created and allowed for the observation of three more planetary bodies: Uranus, Neptune, and Pluto. When they made these discoveries, they continued with the Greek/Roman god theme, assigning the planets their names in relation to this ancient mythology. They named their innermost new discovery, the new seventh planet from the sun, Uranus, unchanged from the Greek, one of the original two gods, alongside Gaia, the earth goddess. Uranus is very similar to the archetypal concept of yang, being the prototypical male energy. Neptune, a blue planet, was named for the Greek god Poseidon, ruler of the seas. And finally, the outermost planet in the solar system was named for the ruler of the underworld, Hades. With this simple discovery, our perception of the skies, and astrology, were changed forever, now consisting of eight planetary bodies (nine if you count the earth) instead of five.

The other way in which this list was expanded to ten instead of eight was by including the sun and moon in the list of planetary bodies. Even though they are not planets in the astronomical sense of the word, they are considered so in astrology. So, with the discovery of three new planets, astrology changed forever, now having three more bodies to observe and derive meaning from. For context, we can see the inclusion of the sun and moon in the seven days of the week, which were named after the seven acknowledged planetary bodies. The names have been changed in English, altered by the influence of Norse mythology, but their rough outline is

- Sunday (sun - day)

- Monday (moon - day)

- Tuesday (Mars - day)

- Wednesday (Mercury - day)

- Thursday (Jupiter - day)

- Friday (Venus - day)

- Saturday (Saturn - day)

This is just another example of the importance of the planets in Ancient Greek culture.

Including the planets in our astrological methodology helps us to expand on the facets of ourselves that are influenced by the celestial world. We have already touched on this a bit with sun, moon, and rising signs. As we talked about, a sign being in your sun is very different from a sign being in your moon. The sign will manifest differently given the planetary body that was in that sign. The planets are an extension of this system. Just as the sun and moon pass through certain constellations on their planetary journeys, so too do the planets, albeit in different patterns. Each planet is ruled by a certain emotion or facet of life. On your birth chart, you will also get a description of where all the planets were at the time of your birth. So, beyond your sun, moon, and rising, you will also have what sign your Venus, Mercury, Jupiter, and so on, were in. This can help you add further complexity to your astrological profile, being able to assign the sign you were born under to different planetary categories and compartmentalizing the way you think about your position within the zodiac. In this pillar, we will be examining all ten of these planetary bodies in great detail, explaining their relationship to astrology and the zodiac.

# Chapter 6:
## Inner Planets

In our exploration of how the planets work in astrology, we will be starting with the first five planets on the list, or the "inner planets." These are the planets that are closest to the earth and thus are the brightest when we look at the night sky. These inner planets are the sun, the moon, Mercury, Venus, and Mars. The main difference between the inner and outer planets is their degree of influence and the type of influence that they have. Inner planets have a more immediate effect on your individual life, pertaining to personal issues like your relationships, career, and even personality. This distinction between the levels of planets has more to do with their degree of orbit than their distance from earth. The further out a planet is, the longer its orbit, and thus the slower it will move through the zodiac. For example, Mercury has an 88-day orbit, meaning that it moves through the zodiac at around four times the speed of the earth. This means that the week of the year you were born will define your Mercury position, and therefore everyone's will be quite varied. Pluto, on the other hand, takes 248 years to orbit the sun, meaning that it only enters a different zodiac sign every 20 years. This means that each generation will have its own distinct Pluto sign. So, you see how the inner and outer planets have more connection to the individual versus the collective. While inner planets have the ability to influence individual lives, outer planets can influence generations. Here is a list of all the inner planets and their significance in the zodiac.

## The Sun

The sun needs no introduction. It is the center of the solar system—although not in the Greek geocentric model—and the force that dominates our skies. It creates day and night and nourishes crops so we have food to eat. As we have discussed in earlier sections, the sun of your zodiac sign is the most important and overarching. It is usually the sign people identify themselves as when asked, constructing their base zodiacal identity around their sun sign. Almost every other sign on your chart will be filtered through your sun sign. If you tell an astrologer your moon or any other planet, they will likely also need your sun in order to give you a proper interpretation. As in the real world, the sun rules all.

## The Moon

As we also talked about back in Chapter 2, the moon on your chart represents the inner self, the person you are under the facade you show to the world. It is characterized by emotions, instinct, and inner reasoning. Your moon sign will reflect not only who you are on the inside but also how you see yourself. For this reason, the moon is very important for inner work, even in relation to other people.

# Mercury

Now we start on the planets, the ones we have not talked about previously. Each of these planets will have a specific area in which they influence your life. In Mercury's case, it's the intellectual world. The sign that is in Mercury for you will heavily influence the way you speak, write, and, above all, pursue knowledge. Because everyone will have a Mercury sign, and all signs will behave differently when in Mercury, you need not be an intellectual person in the conventional sense of the word to have a Mercury value. Everyone communicates and pursues knowledge, just not necessarily in the same ways. You might pursue knowledge through reading, talking to others, or even moving your body. Everyone has a unique intelligence that can be seen in different ways. The constellation that Mercury was passing through will influence these things in you no matter the pursuit you choose in life.

As with any other aspect of the zodiac, Mercury has its good sides and bad sides. Negative relationships with Mercury involve the corruption of intellectual facilities or using intelligence to hurt or deceive others. These involve trickery, conning people, or simply outsmarting others for personal gain. Those who have more aggressive or ambitious signs in Mercury should watch out that they don't fall prey to these kinds of temptations. When manifested positively, Mercury can be the sign of great intellectual power. Those who have strong relationships with Mercury, or more empathetic signs in Mercury, will instead use their powers to help others, such as through teaching or artistic accomplishments. Manifesting a positive relationship with Mercury will help you harness this planet's amazing powers for good.

So, what are some examples of how different zodiac signs might manifest in the Mercury position? Regardless of your sun or moon signs, the sign that Mercury falls under will rule your intellectual side. So, you might be one sign in your sun, moon, and rising, but if you have your Mercury in another sign, that sign will rule your academic pursuits. For example, say you have your Mercury in Leo. Regardless of your other signs, you will probably be a pretty ambitious thinker. You might take a lot of pride in your intelligence and seek out recognition from others even though you might be shy in other areas. Mercury Leos make amazing innovators because they will stop at nothing to make a name for themselves in the intellectual world. If your Mercury is in Aquarius, however, you might have a really avant-garde approach to intelligence. You might seek out new or experimental literature or music. Mercury Aquarians are born artists. They are able to present as totally weird with the intelligence to back it all up. You'll likely find a Mercury Aquarius setting up their latest art installation or trying to make their way through *Finnegan's Wake.* These are just a few examples of how the signs might manifest in Mercury.

## Venus

Venus, the planet of love, unsurprisingly dictates your approach to romantic relationships and even passion in general. The sign that Venus is in will indicate powerful things about your love life. What is interesting about your Venus position is that it doesn't just describe you, but the people you are attracted to as well. As much as Venus indicates what you are like in love, it can also be a strong indicator of what you are looking for in a partner. Another interesting thing about Venus is that, because of the orbital nature of the planet and its relationship to the earth, it does not stray far from the sun. Therefore, your Venus will always be either the same as your sun sign or one immediately beside your sun sign. Those with both their sun and Venus in the same sign will likely experience smoother love lives where they are able to understand their romantic self more easily since it runs so similarly to their core self. Those with differing Venuses and suns might have a little trouble in the early days of their romantic life, figuring out the different side of themselves that comes out when they are in a relationship. A smaller side of Venus is your general hedonistic or materialistic side—the things that bring you comfort or material fulfillment.

The positive and negative sides of Venus can be somewhat polarizing. On one hand, Venus can be a lackadaisical planet if it's interacting with the wrong sign. Venus is pliant and therefore very easily swayed. If it is mixed with a mutable sign, then you can run the risk of becoming excessively passive, especially in love. You might also risk becoming too hedonistic or excessive, consuming too much good food or luxury items for your own good. Venuses in more passive or excessive signs need to learn to control themselves in order to resist always giving in to their desires. On the good side, Venus can manifest as wonderfully decadent and passionate. Having a more giving sign in the Venus position can allow you to share your excesses with others, turning hedonism into a party! More loving signs in Venus will create some of the best lovers possible as their Venus energies are perfectly aligned. For the Venus position, it's all about controlling and outwardly projecting your desires.

Let's look at some examples of how certain signs might manifest under Venus. To start, if you have your Venus in Aries, you will be one of the most intense lovers imaginable. You might be drawn to competition in love, perhaps preferring to pursue people who are already in relationships or are playing hard to get. You see love as a conquest, but be careful not to see your lover as a prize. Remembering that there is still a relationship to be nurtured after it is achieved will help the Aries Venus stay in control of their intense fantasies. If you have your Venus in Libra, then you are especially vulnerable to the passive side of Venus. You might be prone to letting your partner make all the decisions, never really making any for yourself. Libra Venuses should find ways to harness their inner desires in order to have a voice for themselves. These are just a few ways in which your Venus position could be manifested under some signs.

# Mars

While Venus represents passive energy, Mars represents all action. Your Mars sign will therefore represent your relationship to activity, competition, and ambition. How you act when faced with a rival will be dictated by your Mars position. How you plan your career goals might also correspond to your Mars sign. And finally, the way in which you pursue daily action versus passivity has a strong relationship to Mars. Since everyone has a Mars position, even the meekest among us, it does not necessarily indicate that you *are* a competitive person, but rather the degree of your competitiveness and how you go about it. Having a less competitive sign in Mars will indicate that you approach competition from a more laid-back perspective or even avoid it altogether. These planet positions indicate that everyone has a relationship with all facets of life and that even trying not to have a relationship with something is still some kind of a relationship after all.

The positive and negative aspects of Mars are strongly related to the positive and negative aspects of the Aries sign. If you have too fiery or strong of a sign in Mars, you will likely struggle with your competitiveness. You might become a chronic game player or a sore loser. You might overexert yourself, prioritizing constant action over taking a break. Having a more toned-down sign in Mars will indicate that you have a more passive, or potentially healthier, relationship with competition and action. Those with more mutable or even fixed signs in Mars will be able to strike a balance, possibly enjoying a mildly active life or some friendly competition once in a while but never taking it too far.

Mars is an interesting planet in the zodiac because it has a clear sign equivalent: Aries, which is derived from the same Greek god of war. Having your Mars in Aries obviously indicates a harmony where your competitive side can reach its full potential. For this reason, it might seem hard to picture how other signs can interact, but it actually works quite smoothly. If you have your Mars in Cancer, this might mean that your active or competitive side is very focused on your loved ones. You might be the kind of person who would drive three hours to help a friend whose car broke down or spend hundreds of dollars at a carnival game to win your significant other a prize. Cancer Marses are lovers who go all the way. On the flip side, you might have your Mars in Virgo, which can manifest as being extremely controlling or even overworking yourself at the expense of other important aspects of life. If you have your Virgo in Mars, you really need to make sure that you keep your work ethic in check, otherwise, you might end up sacrificing other important aspects of your life for the sake of ambition. From these examples, we can see how Mars often takes certain aspects of a sign to the extreme.

# Chapter 7:
# Outer Planets

As we move outward in the solar system, we are moving toward more big-picture ideas. Thinking back to our explanation of the inner and outer planet dichotomy, we can remember that the farther away from the sun a planet is, the wider its scope becomes, and the longer the orbit of the planet is, the more people that sign has influence over and the more it can define eras. In this chapter, we will discuss the qualities of the outer planets, demonstrating their most important qualities and how they interact with the signs.

## Jupiter

The largest planet in the solar system, Jupiter occupies a transitional position in the planet zodiac. Although it is categorized as an outer planet, it is still related to the individual. However, it occupies an interesting position pertaining to an individual's relationship with the higher world at large. Jupiter is all about higher causes, spiritual and charitable pursuits, and honesty. Your sign in Jupiter represents how you connect to the world as a whole and enact these personal philosophies. Where your

Jupiter falls will dictate your feelings about things like religion—organized or not—and altruism. This planet bridges the gap between the individual and the collective. Your Jupiter sign will indicate your degree of solemnity about life and your level of obligation toward others.

Though Jupiter might sound like a sign that is all good, there is bad in it too. Signs who tend too much toward traditionalism or judgment might end up becoming religious extremists under Jupiter. Signs with a lot of pride might end up being smug or self-righteous about their charity, whether it is religious or not. Remember to connect with *why* you are helping others or pursuing spiritual questions and try to keep your ego out of it as best you can. On the other hand, signs that lean toward caring deeply will be greatly exaggerated under Jupiter. They might be able to finally break out of their shells and create something beautiful or help lots of people in a meaningful way. If Jupiter and its sign are aligned, these people make amazing philosophers, nuns or monks, and poets. Able to devote themselves fully to exploring the mysteries beyond, they can go very far.

Jupiter will manifest very differently within different signs. In Sagittarius, Jupiter might create an outgoing version of charity in a person's life. They might pursue giving charity and altruism by connecting with others. They will be the kind of person to start a food drive or yoga class, searching for ways to bring people together toward higher and noble causes. With their social butterfly skills, they will be more than capable of banding people together and reminding them of the true meaning of caring. In Taurus, however, some of the values of Jupiter might get lost. Jupiter Tauruses might find themselves caught up in bureaucracy, forgetting that true meaning is found in the little things. They might find themselves delaying their goals in life in favor of things like stability, perhaps continually putting off traveling, having children, or even creative pursuits until they feel they have gained enough traction in their careers. Taurus Jupiters should remind themselves that the best things in life are free and true fulfillment doesn't necessarily come from hard work, just love. Clearly, Jupiter is a highly variable planet, with every sign taking its own interpretations of its vague values of truth and benevolence.

# Saturn

Previously considered the "evil" planet of the chart, Saturn is connected to limitation and rigidity. But these things aren't always bad. In fact, everyone needs some limitations in order to succeed in life. You can think of Saturn's limitations like the structure of a sonnet. Instead of limiting the sonneteer with its strict 14 lines and iambic pentameter, it opens up a wide variety of possibilities for the poet to create endless art through a very structured medium. The sign that is in Saturn for you will represent your approach to limitations and planning. It might reflect how you schedule yourself or whether you are more methodical or free-spirited. As with all the planets, Saturn deals in degrees, helping you to see where you fall on the scale in relation to a certain category. Depending on what sign your Saturn is in, or even what your sun or moon signs are, you will have a different approach to planning.

As we said above, the qualities of Saturn can be very good in some regards. Planning is needed to have a fruitful life. You can't always just wing everything. Similarly, you have to limit yourself sometimes, otherwise, you can become too hedonistic or carefree. The qualities of Saturn keep you grounded. Of course, too much limitation can bog you down as well, closing doors on exciting possibilities that might have been within your grasp. You don't want too strict of a sign in Saturn or you might find yourself living a repressed and rigid lifestyle. Striking a balance is the most important thing about Saturn.

The sign that is most obvious to place in Saturn is Capricorn. Because of their hardworking and driven nature, Capricorns are given to depriving themselves of things they don't see as relevant to their goals. They limit and streamline their lives. If your Saturn is in Capricorn, you must make sure not to become too regimented and learn to stop and smell the roses once in a while. On the other hand, if your Saturn is in Pisces, this might mean that you are mainly regimented about your emotions. You might have a certain kind of relationship that you think you "should" have and, consequently, avoid all others because they might not fit your mold. You might even become emotionally repressed, refusing to feel certain things that you don't deem acceptable. Like Saturn in Capricorn, Pisces Saturns should learn to loosen up a little bit and allow themselves to feel whatever they are feeling.

## Uranus

Uranus symbolizes truth and renewal, even revolution. The sign that Uranus is in will reflect the area of your life or yourself that you feel is most subject to radicalism or change. This might mean that this facet of your life will undergo some massive upheaval at some point during your life, or it may even be an area where you are particularly honest or rebellious. This can be good or bad. On one hand, this could mean something catastrophic like a devastating breakup or divorce, the death of a loved one, or a major job loss. On the other hand, it could mean an international move, finding love later in life, or changing your career path to something that brings you more fulfillment and joy. The possibilities are endless, but you can be assured that wherever Uranus falls, this will never be a stable or boring part of your life!

Obviously, destruction can be a force for good and bad. In Hinduism, there is a very important god devoted to this concept. Shiva, the god of destruction and renewal, is symbolized by fire and denotes that though destruction may be painful or difficult on the surface, it is necessary for new things to form. Just like death is necessary to make way for new life, winter is necessary to make way for spring, and night is necessary to make way for day, the world is made up of cycles of death and rebirth. This concept is also important in Tarot. The common sitcom joke of the Death card actually being good is based on truth. Cards like Death, the Tower, or the Hanged Man all symbolize how destruction, death, and even seeing things from a new perspective are all necessary for experiencing renewal in life. You might get the Tower card before a major career change, symbolizing the death of your routines and relationships with colleagues at your old workplace to make way for a new routine, new friends, a new place, and even a new personality. You can think of Uranus as being similar to these tarot cards or the god Shiva—a force of destruction that can bring about growth.

If your Uranus is in, say, Cancer, then the upheavals you might experience will be connected to family and friends, those close, homey relationships. This might be a precarious position to be in. It could symbolize a rocky home life but also one that values authenticity above all else. Even though you might not have the most stable relationships, you will never be in an inauthentic one. You will always value living your truth with others and won't suffer any fools who try to change you. If your Uranus is in Scorpio, then the massive changes to your life might be internal. You might change political affiliations or religions at some point in your life. You will also always be true to yourself in terms of your internal life. You might have a hard time lying to yourself and will always put in the hard work of evaluating whether you truly believe something. Denial is not a familiar state for those with their Uranus in Scorpio. So you see, whatever area you have in Uranus will be rife with change but also realness.

# Neptune

Neptune exists exclusively in the realm of the ideal. Neptune represents your dreams and the things you want to explore in your life. Because Neptune is the Roman god of the sea (the equivalent to the Greek god of the sea, Poseidon), the planet Neptune's qualities are related to the flowing, mysterious sea. If you are familiar with the concept of Platonic ideals, then you will have an idea of how the sign Neptune works. The sign that your Neptune is in will have a strong connection to your ideals and deepest wishes for your life. It will cover both the sphere to which you attach the most romanticism or idealism as well as the way you go about pursuing these ideals. Depending on what sign your Neptune falls in, you might be more or less of a romantic or idealistic person, or your idealism may just manifest in a different way.

There are of course pros and cons to the Neptune sign. On one hand, people who are too strong in their Neptune might fall prey to too much idealism. This can manifest in one of two ways. It can either make you excessively dreamy, too distracted by your made-up world to focus on what's actually happening, or it can cause you frustration, believing in your ideals so much that the real world never measures up and you are forever unsatisfied. However, a lot of good can still come from having a strong Neptune in your chart. For one, those with particularly creative or industrious signs in Neptune are apt to be amazing artists or writers. They have strong connections to their imaginations and have a remarkable ability to bring what they see in their mind's eye onto the page. This is the visionary planet, the one that allows us to see past the physical world and into those unfathomable things beyond.

Different signs will have a huge impact on how Neptune manifests, some more positive than others. Having your Neptune in Gemini, for example, might create an excessively dreamy personality. Because

Gemini is an air sign and prone to some shallowness, Neptune in Gemini can easily create a person who comes across as too flaky or too caught up in their dreams. Gemini Neptunes have to be very careful how they conduct themselves and would do well to have some strong earth signs elsewhere in their chart to help ground them. Having your Neptune in Virgo, however, will create a very interesting person. Combining idealism and creativity with a methodological disposition will form a very industrious artist. You might find a Virgo Neptune planning out an elaborate fantasy book series with complex worlds or making huge oil paintings with meticulous detail. Virgo in Neptune forms the perfect balance to create a visionary, but productive, thinker.

# Pluto

In charge of more grand archetypes, Pluto is the planet of change and the relationship between the ego and the collective. It represents grand transformation in one or another facet of life. It can also be related to sexuality and power, even money. The sign that is in Pluto will shape the way in which these things manifest. If there is a particularly un-orthodox or restless sign in Pluto, then this signifies a life or period of time of significant change. However, if there is a meek or subtle sign in Pluto, then these changes might be more internal or underground in the person or culture. The sign also might signify how you react to change or how change is enacted by you. It all depends on the level of confidence of the sign.

The planet with the most widespread influence will be Pluto since entire generations share the same Pluto sign. If you look back on Pluto's schedule, you can see how it could possibly have had an influence on that generation's sensibilities. For example, Pluto was in Leo from 1937 to roughly 1958, which are generally the defining years of the "Baby

Boomer" generation. This generation was known for confidence, pride, and paving their own path. They were sometimes referred to as the "me" generation by their parents, possibly reflecting their intense individualism. All having their Pluto in Leo suggests that that generation was given to more bold, individualistic, and passionate thinking, which reflects in the sexual revolution, the large number of social movements during the time, and the general prosperity they experienced. It seems like the Baby Boomers achieved a lot of their goals, still to this day remaining the wealthiest and most successful generation in history.

Those born from 1958 to 1972, on the other hand, all had their Plutos in Virgo. The intense hard work and often disappointing success levels of their generation ("Generation X") are reflected in this. Gen Xers are known for being unlucky economically, graduating into depression, and having less professional prosperity than their parents. We can see how Virgo's more frugal nature is reflected in this. Finally, those born from 1995 to 2008, or "Generation Z," have their Plutos in Sagittarius. Given the more charitable and equitable nature of Sagittarius, we can see how the deep devotion to social movements and inclusivity, along with extreme anger toward inequality, are reflected in Gen Z's Pluto-Sagittarius position. As we can see, Pluto has clearly influenced some defining aspects of certain generations throughout the 20th and 21st centuries. Who knows what those born in the current stage, Pluto in Capricorn, will bring to the world?

# Chapter 8:
## Chiron Planet

Another astronomical phenomenon that has an important place in astrology is the newly discovered Chiron. Chiron was first spotted in 1977 and has since undergone many reclassifications. First, it was classified as an outer planet, then an asteroid, and now a comet. It exists among the outer planets of the solar system, just between Saturn and Uranus. It has since been introduced as an important player among the celestial bodies in astrology, especially since its discovery coincided with the height of the new age movement when astrology was being profoundly redefined. Its location right in between Saturn and Uranus, two completely opposite planets, positions Chiron as a kind of mediator between the two. Since Saturn is the planet of restriction and Uranus the planet of breaking free, Chiron lies somewhat in the middle, helping to bridge the full spectrum of emotions.

# What Does Chiron Symbolize?

Chiron is, simply put, the celestial body of healing. Its name comes from a famous Ancient Greek healer with a tragic story. He had immense powers to heal other people yet was sick himself and could not heal his own ailments. His story represents that, while many people have the ability to recognize flaws in others and even help them heal, it can be much more difficult to recognize your own faults and begin to heal yourself. The planet Chiron represents this contradiction. Thus, it works toward the process of using our own pain to heal others, of recognizing in ourselves what might be wrong and then sharing those findings so others can learn from them. Among these things, Chiron also stands for your own healing as well, if you choose to meet it. Periods of Chiron healing are opportunities to truly investigate the depths of your pain psyche, paving the way for transformative change. If you allow your Chiron sign and cycle to fully enter you, then you will be able to heal from many of the things that have brought you pain throughout your life. The process won't be easy, but the results will be beyond amazing.

# The Chiron Cycle

As with the ten planetary bodies, Chiron has its own schedule for how it moves through the zodiac. First of all, its complete rotation takes roughly 50 years. This is the amount of time it takes to go all the way around the sun and return to its original position. This means that Chiron is in a different sign every four years. The complete cycle is very important to your life cycle. The phase Chiron is in during your birth will shape the rest of your life. When it comes around again, roughly at your 50th birthday, this is a time of profound change. Sometimes this is called a "midlife crisis," but it doesn't have to be a crisis. It can be a period of learning and growth.

When your Chiron returns, you will be able to confront many of your core qualities. You will be under the influence of its original sign, and thus it will feel like a full circle or a homecoming to you. Many people use this time to make serious reevaluations of major things in their lives, like marriages, careers, friendships, personal style, and more. You might notice your 50th birthday as a turning point where you either start to feel more lost and disconnected or begin to shed the excesses and live a more authentic life. Those who choose to ignore the insights of their Chiron return might double down on their illusions and continue on their existing path, purposefully blinding themselves to the inauthenticity or discomfort of some aspects of their life. Those who choose to embrace it, though, will find themselves in a state of destruction and renewal. You might have to end relationships or career paths, but what you will be left with is a more honest way forward, a new life that will allow you to shed all the excess you have accumulated over the years and truly start to be your authentic self.

One way you can help yourself harness the power of the Chiron cycle is to take a close look at all aspects of your life and really ask yourself whether these are the things you want to be doing. A small way to start is by decluttering. Many people have far too many things in their homes, so taking some time to throw out or give away some of those extra things you don't need can leave you feeling renewed and refreshed. Another way is to make a list of the goals you have for the rest of your life and to ask yourself whether the path you are currently on is one where you will be able to accomplish those goals. You might also want to see a counselor or open up to a close friend to start having some of these deep conversations with another person. If you are able to navigate this transitional period, then you will be able to live out the rest of your life feeling more honest and authentic.

# Chiron and the Signs

So, how does your sign manifest in Chiron? The way the signs are typically talked about in relation to Chiron is through wounds and healing strategies. Every sign will have both a pain point (something with which they will struggle throughout their lives) and a healing point (their way of sharing their wisdom with others). Depending on the sign your Chiron is in, you will have a very different relationship to emotional pain and suffering as well as a totally different method of dealing with it. Here, we will look at the ways the 12 zodiac signs interact with the Chiron.

## Aries

Those born under the sign of Aries are born with the implicit pain of always channeling their emotions into anger. Almost every feeling an Aries experiences is turned into anger. This means they will have a big problem harnessing their anger because so much of what they experience turns into it. Anger management is thus one of the biggest issues for the Aries Chiron. Aries Chirons might also struggle with self-worth, unable to see what is so great about themselves even though other people might be able to see it easily. Finally, their cutthroat approach to competition is likely to make them feel lonely. They might cut people out of their lives in pursuit of being the best. If they do this, though, they will soon realize that it can be very lonely at the top.

However, Aries Chirons can show other people some amazing things. The best gift that Aries Chirons can give those around them is showing them how amazing they are and building their confidence. If an Aries's energy is channeled properly, they can be the ultimate cheerleaders. They will especially empower others to embrace their unique qualities and be unashamedly themselves. They might also be able to channel their anger more creatively, using all that energy to make something extraordinary. If you have a well-adjusted Chiron Aries in your life, they will help you make many amazing discoveries about yourself.

## Taurus

Chiron in Taurus will struggle primarily with stubbornness and rigidity. They will likely fear change to the point of avoiding important transitions in life, possibly entering a state of arrested development at some point. They might struggle to move out of their parents' house when they are young or to request a promotion at work when they are older. Taurus Chirons also might fall into the trap of going with the crowd rather than forming their own distinct opinions. They might find themselves joining organized religion or politics more easily without really considering whether it is what they actually believe. They might also be given to materialism, potentially squandering their skills in pursuit of money alone and losing sight of meaning in their lives. All these faults and points of pain are very common among Taurus Chirons.

There are also very important gifts associated with Taurus Chirons. For one, they are exceptional at creating comforting environments for those around them. They always know what makes someone feel good, so they will almost magically be able to provide that exact thing you didn't even know you were lacking. They will also be the ones to keep their cool in a crisis. You will never see a Taurus Chiron panicking—they always find a way to stay calm in any circumstance. For this reason, they make great emergency service people since they aren't easily shaken. Finally, they are also excellent planners, especially when it comes to money. You can learn a lot from the way this sign deals with their finances. Therefore, despite the flaws listed above, Taurus Chirons also have many important things going for them.

## Gemini

Because Gemini is the sign of twinship and companionship, their main point of pain will be fear of abandonment or loneliness. Geminis may become extremely distressed or volatile if they fear that someone might be leaving them or that they might end up alone. They might resort to groveling or people-pleasing behavior where they sacrifice their own comfort for the placation of someone else. Because of this, Gemini Chirons often end up suppressing their true selves because of their intense fear of not being liked. Another major difficulty Gemini Chirons might struggle with is a tendency toward flakiness and being unable to finish what they started. Unfinished projects will often litter the homes of Gemini Chirons, who tend to be able to muster the energy to start things only to lose interest halfway through. This is the wispiness of the air infiltrating the minds of these Gemini Chirons.

Yet, when channeled in the right way, Gemini Chirons can be some of the most amazing people in the world. They will particularly shine in the social world, dominating teaching and inclusivity initiatives. Where Gemini Chirons really excel is in learning through play. They are able to make learning even the driest information a great time because they approach it with a playful curiosity. If you have a Gemini Chiron as your teacher, you will likely not even realize you are learning because you will be having so much fun. They are also amazing at making outsiders feel at ease in social situations. They're the kind of people who will notice the wallflower and make sure they feel included and welcome. At a party with a Gemini Chiron, you can bet that nobody is going to feel left out.

## Cancer

Those with Chiron in Cancer will usually have anxieties and pain centered around security. Cancer Chirons often have heavily fortified homes, possibly with multiple locks on the door or even a guard dog. They might struggle to ever feel like they are secure, piling on security blanket after security blanket to no avail. Due to this borderline paranoia, they might have a particular mistrust of strangers. People they don't know, foreigners, or even people with different belief systems from them might seem suspect in their eyes. Because of their nesting compulsion, Cancer Chirons are also wont to hoard things, such as money or possessions. They might become misers, gluttons, or even full-on hoarders. If they aren't careful, these tendencies can cause their inner space to become even more unstable, leading to family dysfunction.

If the Cancer Chiron is able to turn their "nesting" and security tendencies outward, broadening the circle of those they trust, then they can become amazing community organizers. Cancer Chirons have a wonderful ability to mobilize people in a community toward positive change. They will usually focus on the most vulnerable in the community, possibly people lacking homes or who struggle with mental illness or addiction. The crux is that they are able to see these people as insiders who share their community, which will allow the Cancer Chiron to see this community aid as an extension of their own home. They will also use food as a love language, often making huge batches of recipes and giving out their warm and hearty sustenance to anyone who asks. Finally, Cancer Chirons are incredibly good with money and will budget very well, taking all the people in their life into account.

## Leo

Chiron Leos will struggle with all the main flaws of Leo and more. The pain points of the Leo Chiron are very similar to those of the Aries. They are terrified of not being well-liked or succeeding in their endeavors. Chiron Leos will become very easily frustrated with themselves. Because Leo is known for, and therefore used to, succeeding at things without much effort, failure is devastating. If a Chiron Leo finds that something does not come easily to them, they will either blame themselves and have an identity crisis over their abilities or they will shun the thing they tried and deem it not worth doing. Both situations are bad since they don't involve the necessary growth failure can bring. Leo Chirons might also struggle with an addiction to intense relationships, forgoing commitment in favor of a string of short, overstimulating flings. This might be fun at first, but it can cause them to start feeling empty over time.

Where Leo Chirons really shine in their healing is through the arts. Using their talents for good, Leo Chirons can do great things with creativity. This might mean using their skills to spread an important political message, or it might mean moving a lot of people by creating something beautiful. Either way, they will be able to greatly touch people and even heal them. Their other healing qualities are similar to those of Aries and Gemini. They are amazing at uplifting others and building others' self-confidence. If they are in a team setting, they will be able to work exceptionally well with their teammates, satisfied enough with their collective goals to avoid showing off.

## Virgo

When Chiron is in Virgo, anxiety will rule. The type of anxiety will depend on the person and their other signs, but some of the most common are perfectionism, body dysmorphia, social anxiety, and hypochondria. In terms of perfectionism, this is common for Virgos, but with the Chiron pain point, it can be debilitating. Excessive perfection-ism often leads to withdrawal from the world and an unwillingness to submit things or engage with people unless you are "perfect." Perfec-tionism can also appear through body dysmorphia, obsessing about ap-pearances to the point of delusion. Social anxiety might also plague the Virgo Chiron, being paralyzed by the idea of being judged by others. Finally, Virgo Chirons might also struggle with an obsession with health, leading either to excessive doctor visits or extreme "healthy" lifestyle practices that can border on dangerous if unchecked. Con-versely, Chiron Virgos might turn these anxieties outward and become excessively critical of people, causing them to possibly lose friends.

At their best, Chiron Virgos can be amazing guides. They can provide others with extremely useful structures for living their lives. For this reason, they thrive particularly in advice positions, such as counselors, financial advisors, wedding planners, and any other organizational care position. If you're making plans for your life or an important event, you'll want no one but a Chiron Virgo helping you. They also can be very wise when it comes to helping others. You might be surprised that a Chiron Virgo who seems a bit neurotic could give you such clear-headed advice. Finally, Chiron Virgos are great communicators and thus can create pieces of writing, media campaigns, and other types of communications that can truly move and inspire people. They are undoubtedly the communicators of the signs.

## Libra

The core of all Libra Chirons' struggles is indecisiveness. When Libra Chirons are in pain, it's almost always because they are unable to confront something or make a clear decision. This creates a real rock-and-a-hard-place situation for the Libra Chiron. On one hand, they are incredibly afraid of commitment. They might not be willing to definitively choose a partner until it's too late and the person has gotten fed up. This indecisiveness might end up losing them many relationship opportunities because they failed to choose when the time came. However, on the other hand, Libras are terrified of conflict and thus often get stuck in unfulfilling relationships because they are unwilling to deal with the confrontation of breaking up. Relationships are where Libra Chirons really feel the brutality of their confrontation anxieties and indecisive natures.

But when they are able to look outward to others, Libra Chirons can truly foster harmony and community wherever they go. For this reason, they are amazing diplomats. They have a remarkable ability to mediate even the most difficult of conflicts, helping people who might be completely opposed eventually see eye to eye. This helpfulness and mediation might also manifest in a romantic way. Libra Chirons are known for carrying messages between lovers, like Friar Lawrence in *Romeo and Juliet*. They find joy in bringing people together, whether in politics, love, or even friendship.

## Scorpio

The dark sign of Scorpio might find some truly difficult anxieties with Chiron. At their worst, Scorpio Chirons are given to nihilism. They might struggle to find meaning in life and end up plain giving up. This is especially common among younger Scorpio Chirons, but it can also happen to older people, especially after a destabilizing life change. The other problem Scorpio Chirons tend to struggle with is jealousy over love or power. They might be particularly jealous partners and can even become possessive if they don't keep it in check. Like Libra suns, they might also have trouble getting out of unfulfilling relationships.

On the flip side, Scorpio Chirons can do a lot for others in terms of deep soul-searching because they are all about the deepest parts of the human soul. If you are contemplating deep questions about yourself, your close relationships, or even your place in the world, no one will be able to guide you through those things better than a Scorpio Chiron. They are especially good at helping people through difficult or transitional times. Scorpio Chirons might, for this reason, seem like "foul-weather friends," or people who seem to always be around when the going gets tough. Births, deaths, major moves—you can bet your Scorpio Chiron friend will be right there with you. For this reason, they are excellent as grief counselors or divorce lawyers, dedicating their lives to the messier parts of other people.

## Sagittarius

In their more negative states, Sagittariuses are very prone to dogmatic or even cult-like thinking. They might be particularly vulnerable to joining cults or making big dramatic changes in their ideology at the drop of a hat. They are the kind of people who can go from being an extreme atheist to a devout believer in a matter of months. Pair this with their extreme wanderlust and tendency toward a nomadic lifestyle, and they are very vulnerable to a cultish lifestyle. They will leave their homes on a whim in search of their next thrill, possibly sacrificing important relationships or good situations. They might also be flippant with others, not really acknowledging the deeper implications of the things they are saying or downplaying the significance of certain relationships. A tendency to abandon or shirk responsibility will always follow them.

But turn them outward, and a Saggitarius Chiron will be a magnetic and electric personality. They will always be able to crack the right joke to lighten even the most somber of circumstances. They are also able to impart wisdom to others with genuine compassion. If they're the ones to tell you about something major in your life, then you can be assured that they will use all the care and consideration in their heart to try to make it acceptable to you. Sagittarius Chirons are also known for producing great creative works, excelling particularly in the field of socially conscious art.

## Capricorn

Capricorn Chirons can't help but be obsessed with their careers. On the most negative side, the Capricorn Chiron is pursuing professional success with the goal of attaining money, completely disregarding the ideas of personal fulfillment or contribution to society. They can easily fall into high-power, high-status positions that might be morally dubious or lack anything creative or personally satisfying. The Capricorn Chiron is thus at risk for deep dissatisfaction with their professional life, failing to understand why they feel discontented since their values are misaligned with their happiness. Usually, this will ricochet into the family, causing strife or even dysfunction in the home.

If the Capricorn Chiron is able to use their talents to help others, they will find themselves to be much more fulfilled. Instead of using status to better themselves, they will instead turn their hard work into something that benefits the community. They will particularly shine as leaders with their go-getter attitudes, making strides and ensuring that everyone gets what they need. Capricorn Chirons can also demonstrate an intense environmental consciousness.

## Aquarius

The rebellious nature of the Aquarius is only made more destructive under Chiron. While their unconventional natures can be a positive thing, even sparking social change, Aquarius Chirons can become rebellious for the mere sake of being so. These rebels without a cause might bring about undue damage to others by refusing to think about consequences. Somewhat contradictorily, Aquarius Chirons also have a tendency to try to fit in with the crowd, especially if they perceive that crowd as unique or exciting. For these two reasons in tandem, Aquarius Chirons are most at risk during their youth when peer pressure around doing drugs, skipping school, or committing petty crimes is at its highest. In adulthood, this desire to fit in with the cool crowd might manifest in them shirking major responsibilities until a mature age or refusing to settle down. They might also be somewhat emotionally detached.

Because of their disregard for the status quo, Aquarius Chirons can do a lot to help others through social justice. They have a strong sense of fairness and right and wrong, so they will never let a group of people be silenced, offering themselves up as spokespeople for the disenfranchised. Whether or not they belong to the group they are protecting, they will fight just as fiercely. Their idealistic natures will help them shine a light on many issues and help people in need.

## Pisces

The emotional and imaginative nature of the Pisces means that the main issue they will face in life will be a divergence from reality. The Pisces Chiron tends to experience difficulty with hard or adult situations, preferring to shy away from the darker parts of the world and live in a more dreamlike state. They might experience intense denial or distress when anything difficult happens to them as they lack the emotional skills to process it adequately. They will often seek out escapism, creating a life in which they don't have to think about unpleasant things. They might also have trouble setting boundaries with other people, becoming stuck in negative cycles they are too timid to break.

On the other hand, they possess strong spiritual skills when it comes to other people. They are the best people to go to for advice on metaphysical or emotional problems. They will still live in fantasy, but because of this, they are amazing at helping you access the core of what you really want. If you're a particularly repressed person, a Pisces Chiron will be the best person to help you unravel those repressed feelings and unlock what your true desires are. Pisces Chirons are so good at these things that they can sometimes veer into the psychic. Many fortune tellers or psychics are Pisces Chirons because of their acute perceptive abilities and their alignment with the spiritual world.

# Chapter 9:
# Retrograde Planets

Besides the individual planets themselves, there are also specific states a planet can be in that will affect its meaning. The most common one of these states is retrograde. Retrograde is when a planet is moving backward through the night sky, opposite to its usual course. Whether or not a planet in your chart is in retrograde greatly affects its meaning. In fact, a planet in retrograde might completely change that planet's meaning, and in turn, its effect on you. Retrograde in astrology is somewhat similar to reversed cards in the Tarot. If a card is in the upside-down position in a Tarot reading, then its meaning will be the opposite. Retrograde, however, is somewhat more complicated than Tarot reversals, creating a very specific change in meaning. In this chapter, we will talk all about retrograde and how it can have an effect on your chart.

# How Does Retrograde Happen?

Retrograde is a well-documented astrological phenomenon. Astrologers have charted retrogrades since the dawn of time. Before the heliocentric model (i.e., the sun as the center of the solar system instead of the earth), retrogrades appeared merely as the planets acting up. Thus, astronomers began to think of these retrogrades as the planets "acting out of character," or contradicting their natures. As a result, the concept of astrological retrograde was born.

Once scientists were able to more closely chart the planets as they revolve around the sun, they discovered the true reason that planets retrograde. It is a complex optical illusion caused by the earth and another planet passing each other's orbit. Remember back in the section on the inner planets how I explained that all planets have different orbiting speeds and times? We talked about how Mercury spins the fastest and has the shortest journey while Neptune and Pluto spin the slowest and have the longest journeys. Well, that is important to the concept of retrograde. Because all the planets have different orbiting speeds, they will have to pass each other at some point. When the earth passes another planet, which it does with every single one at some point, that planet momentarily appears to be going much slower, even backward! When you chart the planet's position in the sky, it will appear to not be moving at all, or even moving briefly backward, before regaining its original course and moving forward again. Similar to the orbits, each planet's retrograde will depend on its speed. Mercury has the shortest period of being in retrograde, while Pluto has the longest.

# What Does Retrograde Mean?

So, what does retrograde do to the meaning of the planets? Let's think back for a second to how the planets function in astrology. Each planet has a different meaning or facet of life over which it presides. Its interaction with a particular zodiac sign will determine the person's personality type in relation to that facet. If, however, a planet happens to be in retrograde at the time of your birth, then that meaning will be changed. Therefore, a Mars Gemini will be significantly different from a Mars Gemini retrograde.

The specific way in which retrogrades affect planets is by blocking or obscuring their meaning. It transforms the meaning of the planet from the outside or core world to the inner world. In a way, planets are to their retrogrades as the sun is to the moon. You will experience the same personality profiles as the sign, just on an inner or more hidden level. So, while a Leo Venus might have a very bold and show-offy attitude toward romance, a Leo Venus retrograde will still have that attitude but will hide it from the world. They might only want to do big romantic gestures in the privacy of their home or only show their deeply romantic side after they've really gotten to know someone. You can think of retrogrades as sort of putting the planet's meaning in shadow, relegating it to a more private or deeply felt arena.

# Which Planets Are in Retrograde?

All of the planets orbiting the sun have the potential to be in retrograde and go through a scheduled retrograde period at their appointed times. However, I did say that the term "planets" in astrology technically referred to the sun and moon as well. This is not the case for retrogrades. Since the sun and moon are on distinct orbiting paths, they cannot experience retrograde. They each have their own internal cycles of things such as lunar and solar eclipses which affect their meanings, but retrograde isn't something that applies to them. For the purposes of retrograde, "planet" is used with the conventional meaning: the eight (or nine, if you count the earth) celestial bodies that orbit the sun.

## How Retrograde Affects Each Planet

Because every planet has a different meaning, retrograde will affect them all differently. Some planets involve a very fundamental part of life, making their retrogrades particularly tricky. Other planets might already deal with a very internal or private area of life, which can cause them to become excessively insular. The other thing that will affect the planets is their retrograde schedule. Planets like Mercury and Venus go through very rapid and frequent retrogrades, while the outer planets can be in retrograde for months. Thus, the inner planets' retrogrades will be more randomly dispersed, while there can be whole half-years worth of people who have the same Pluto in retrograde, leading to more significant numbers of people. Here, we will look at how retrograde affects the meaning of each planet in the solar system.

### Mercury

So, I have actually lied to you so far. Technically, Mars and Venus don't go through a conventional retrograde. Because these planets are both closer to the sun than the earth, they experience a slightly different version of retrograde. They pass the earth, but the earth does not pass them, so it won't look the same as a Mars or Jupiter retrograde. However, the effect on astrological charting is still the same, so they are important to consider.

Mercury is the most common planet to be in retrograde. For this reason, a lot of people have Mercury retrograde in their charts. Because Mercury is related to intellectual pursuits, having your Mercury in retrograde means that you will have a much deeper, more internal intellectual life. You might not be an amazing public speaker, but you will be a voracious reader and have the ability to ponder questions at a deeper level than the average person. You will likely relate everything in your life to something philosophical and might find that you can't help always looking at things through the lens of their deeper meanings.

## Venus

Again, Venus technically does not go through a true retrograde, but the retrograde rules still apply. The planet of love being in retrograde means that your romantic affairs will be much closer to your heart than most. You might have trouble even telling your friends when you have a crush on someone, let alone the person themselves. This can lead to being extremely guarded and having a difficult time really showing love unless you feel incredibly secure. However, this is all made up for by the level of intensity that Venus retrogrades experience in relationships. They often seek a higher level of intimacy than other people and will have some of the closest bonds possible with friends and lovers.

## Mars

Mars is one of the more interesting and difficult to pin down retrogrades. It can manifest in one of two ways. Either the Mars retrograde internalizes their competitive desire to be the best so deeply that they end up trying much harder and becoming aggressive as a result, or the Mars retrograde becomes ashamed of this competitive side and attempts to hide it. Thus, they might come across as the opposite of competitive, comparatively meek and shy. You can think of this side of the retrograde as being somewhat similar to an Aries moon where these competitive desires only come out in specific or private situations.

Either way, Mars retrogrades will struggle with their desires, possibly not recognizing them or taking longer than usual to acknowledge them.

## Jupiter

Jupiter retrogrades have the advantage of being both genuinely imaginative and very good planners. What results is a fascinating person who is able to put even the most far-fetched of goals into action. They will often have a very strong work ethic, believing that hard work is the only thing that can truly lead to a person's success. If they follow these beliefs, then they will certainly go far in life, creating some of the most beautiful and well-planned things ever.

## Saturn

Saturn retrogrades will often have difficulty trusting others. They will struggle with vulnerability, taking a long time before they are able to truly open up to someone else. They might also struggle with guilt, feeling far too much responsibility for their own good and often being severely bothered by things they may feel culpable for but that were outside of their control. And finally, Saturn retrogrades have a very hard time with structure. For them, this goes both ways. They will at once hate anyone trying to impose structure on their lives while also struggling to do so themselves. What results is a highly unstructured life, leading to possible misdirection and feelings of being lost. Saturn retrogrades will need to go through a lot of internal work to overcome these struggles.

## Uranus

As Uranus is the planet of revolution, its retrograde will want to avoid these things while being preoccupied with them at the same time. Uranus retrogrades struggle deeply with the idea of change as it seems to strike a chord deep inside them. They will likely suppress any of their unconventional qualities, which from the outside might make them appear boring or square. But don't be fooled by appearances. Once Uranus retrogrades are comfortable, either alone or with close friends and family, they will let all their wacky energy flow and finally show the world the eccentrics they really are on the inside. They will likely spend their lives in constant strife between order and chaos, convention and rebellion, or repression and release.

## Neptune

Those with the deeply spiritual planet of Neptune in retrograde can be covertly religious. They keep their intense philosophical natures to themselves, preferring to play it cool around other people while housing a strong conviction deep inside. For this reason, Neptune retrogrades might steer away from organized religion, preferring a quiet spirituality that might even be atheistic. If they are involved in organized religion, they will keep this very separate from the rest of their life, perhaps even attending church in a different town to avoid having to worship around people they know. The trademark of a Neptune retrograde is someone who comes across as very laid-back and unserious only to reveal a deeply pious interior.

## Pluto

Those with Pluto in retrograde will probably experience pretty extreme unrest. They will have a lot of contradictions running through them, and because they are in shadow, they will have a hard time unraveling them. Pluto retrogrades will crave yet also fear control and power. They will also hate when someone else has power over them. They will desire power yet also be unaware of this desire and experience frustration around this unnamed craving. And finally, Pluto retrogrades will lack introspection, making them one of the most lost and confused retrogrades out there.

# Pillar 4:
## The Houses

Moving on to the fourth pillar of astrology, we have the houses. Houses in astrology are an entirely different system, separate from the zodiac and the planets. They do, however, bear some distinct similarities. First of all, there are 12 houses, which matches up with the 12 signs in the zodiac. This is purely a superficial similarity since the zodiac is based on the 12 moon cycles and the houses are based on earth's daily rotation, 12 being one-half of the day's 24-hour cycle. They are also similar to the planets in that they preside over different facets of life. So, each house will represent a different part of your life that is also influenced by other astrological factors. In this section on pillar four, we will look at two important elements of the houses. First, in Chapter 10, we will look at each house and give a description of the influence it has over your life. Then, in Chapter 11, we will look at house positions and the impact they have on your birth chart as well.

# Chapter 10:
## Individual Houses

J ust as the signs and planets all have their individual meanings, each house has its own unique meaning as well. There are 12 houses in the zodiac and thus 12 meanings. But how do we calculate these houses? Well, you can think of a house in astrology as being like a slice of the sky. If the entire three-dimensional dome of sky surrounding the earth was divided into 12 slices like an orange, you would get 12 triangular pieces. As the day progresses, we move through all 12 of these houses. Because there are 12 and not 24, the house actually changes every two hours instead of every hour. For this reason, it's necessary to know the exact hour of your birth in order to be able to calculate all your houses. The houses start at the horizon and go up incrementally from there, tied to the location and hour of your birth. When you are born, the constellation (and planet) that is passing through each house will indicate something about it. Though we said that the 12 houses are separate from the zodiac signs astronomically, they are each linked with a corresponding zodiac sign that relates closely to their themes. In this section, we will focus on descriptions of the individual houses.

# First House

Luckily, we already know something about the first house because it is the same as the rising! This house, known as either the first house, the rising, or the ascendant, is the house immediately over the horizon. As we talked about way back in Chapter 2, the rising sign presides over your outward or public self. It is your "mask," or the image you project into the world. Sometimes, this image runs deep, influencing important parts of yourself, and sometimes this image is something you shed the moment you are out of the public sphere. It all depends on the signs and their relation to the first house. The first house is ruled by Aries, reflecting that sign's appearance-based ethos.

# Second House

The second house is all about a person's financial life. Like it or not, everyone has a relationship with the material world. The kinds of bodies occupying the second house will dictate your lifelong relationship with material possessions and wealth. Having a lot of planets in the second house doesn't necessarily indicate that you will be wealthy, though. Rather, they will dictate things like your feelings about money, your luck with money, and the importance monetary success will have to your life. The second house is ruled by Taurus, influenced by that sign's earthiness and staunch practicality.

# Third House

The third house is primarily concerned with communication. Things like talking, writing, traveling, and forming communities will all be covered in the third house. The bodies in your third house will likely dictate your particular communication style, whether it is honest and direct or coy and distant. This house might also dictate your feelings about travel and movement, possibly indicating whether you will be a homebody or full of wanderlust. It will also denote whether you are destined to live in the same place all your life or inclined to move around and see more of the world. Because communication is so central to relationships, professional as well as personal, the third house will also have a bearing on the way you interact with the people in your life on a deeper level. The third house is ruled by Gemini, going with that sign's tendency toward companionship and social skills.

## Fourth House

The fourth house of the sky rules over home and family. This is the house that will reveal answers about the way you operate in a family setting. Certain planets or signs in the fourth house might indicate your specific relationship with your home and family and whether you are someone for whom family is very important or if you are a lone wolf or a wanderer. This house doesn't necessarily have to mean blood family. It could indicate something about your blood family, whether you are involved with them or not, but it could also refer to your adopted, found, or friend family. Any relationship that is tied to your home and inner space falls under the fourth house. Cancer is this house's ruling sign, continuing with Cancer's themes of nurturing and care.

## Fifth House

When you're in the fifth house, it's all about pleasure. But because pleasure has such a wide meaning, the fifth house has a huge variety of life situations over which it presides. Sometimes, philosophers divide pleasures into "high" or "low" pleasures, with low pleasures being things like food or sex and high pleasures being things like taking care of children or learning to play an instrument. However, the fifth house makes no such discrimination and deals with pleasures of all kinds. It sees drinking expensive wine as being on the same level as reading a dense Russian novel or going to a party. Anything that stimulates your senses or makes you feel fulfilled goes under the fifth house. The bodies that interact with the fifth house, however, will determine how you interact with pleasure; how much you allow yourself, how you go about seeking it out, and whether or not you value it in your life. The fifth house's corresponding sign is Leo, given its fiery, egocentric qualities.

## Sixth House

The sixth house deals with health and wellness. More specifically, it refers to the more choice-based aspects of health and wellness. Besides the health qualities you are born with, you also make many choices throughout your life that impact your overall health. The amount of exercise you get, the kinds of foods you eat, and even the strength of your relationships can all contribute to your general health. The sixth house deals with these choices and how they reflect on your mind and body. Thus, whichever bodies are in the sixth house will be reflected in how you feel about and make choices related to your health. It will correspond to whether you are very health-conscious, whether you value mental health more or less than physical health, and whether you are inclined to fulfill your health-based goals. Virgo, with its systematic approach to life, is the equivalent sign to the sixth house.

## Seventh House

Moving into the second half of the houses, we begin to look outward a bit more. The first six houses deal primarily with individual choices, whereas the next six houses focus more on the things that influence you throughout your life. The first of this second half, the seventh house, sits directly opposite the first house. The seventh house is often called the descendant since it is directly opposite the ascendant. The seventh house is mainly focused on transformational relationships in your life. These are the kind of intense, one-on-one relationships that will have an indispensable role in shaping who you are and what you choose to do in life. This is someone more intimate than a teacher or mentor. This kind of relationship is usually with a parent, a very close friend, or a spouse or partner. It will be someone who has seen you at your best and at your worst and seems to know you inside and out. They will feel like a soulmate and someone you can always rely on, shaping the very depths of your soul. Most people will only have a handful of these kinds of relationships throughout their life, so remember to cherish them. Libra is this house's defining sign, ready to allow themselves to be shaped by other influences in the best way possible.

## Eighth House

The eighth house is one of the more intense houses. This is the house of transformation, a mysterious phenomenon that has a few branches. People with a lot of natal planets—or planets at the time of their birth—in the eighth house will be very attracted to the beyond, such as occult practices, astrology, and mysticism. They will seek a place for themselves not just in the real world, but in the order of the universe as well. Other aspects of the eighth house are sex and death, two foundational aspects of life that represent the cycles of creation. There is a reason the French call an orgasm *la petite mort*, or "the little death"—there is certainly something of a rebirth in the sexual experience, linking the two forces of the cycles. The planetary bodies in your eighth house will thus reflect your choices and feelings in regard to these significant forces. The eighth house is ruled by Scorpio's intensely pensive and private nature.

## Ninth House

The ninth house also deals with one's relationship with the world but in a more grounded sense. This house presides over travel and learning. This can either mean a practical form of learning, such as interacting with new people, especially those who live in different cities or countries, or a more internal learning, such as reading challenging books or taking courses. Those with many natal planets in the ninth house will likely value education very highly and pursue many different kinds of knowledge. Of course, which planets those are will dictate the types of intelligence or exploratory pursuits you value the most. Sagittarius, with its love for exploration, rules over the ninth house.

## Tenth House

Another aspect of the latter houses and their focus on the outside world is the status-focused tenth house. While the seventh house focused on intimacy, the eighth house on spiritual belonging, and the ninth house on forging new connections, the tenth house is all about your social identity and status in the world. Having a lot of natal planets in the tenth house will usually mean that you are more ambitious or a social climber. You might value your career or even fame more than some of the more internal qualities of the other houses. The specific bodies in the tenth house will indicate your direction in this socially conscious paradigm. Capricorn's staunch ambition and work ethic rule the tenth house.

## Eleventh House

The eleventh house, in contrast, rules over friendship or the kinds of relationships we have in life that offer us nothing materially but everything emotionally and spiritually. The field of friendship can be broad—it can mean your work friends, your neighbors, your classmates, and of course, those close friends you keep for life. The eleventh house is all about community, surrounding yourself with a network of people who support you and make you feel accepted. For this reason, the eleventh house also has a relationship to humanitarianism and charity as well as innovation. Aquarius and its penchant for both relationships and uniqueness rule the eleventh house.

## Twelfth House

The twelfth house occupies an interesting position in the sky and in the houses: It is just below the horizon and thus invisible. It represents the parts of the self and the universe that are mysterious, unseen, or even unknowable. Dreams and secrets will occupy this house, things that are never spoken aloud or that are even lost to time. If you have a lot of natal planets in the twelfth house, then you will have a strong relationship with the shadow world. You will be able to know things that are hidden from most other people. This might even result in psychic powers. Due to their deeply emotional nature, the twelfth house is ruled by Pisces.

# Chapter 11:
# House Positions

Just as the signs fall under different categories—such as the four elements, the three modalities, or the two polarities—houses too have certain categories under which they fall. You may have noticed some similarities or patterns between certain houses that link them together closely. This isn't a coincidence. There are many houses that share a strong connection with one another. These patterns are called the house positions, and they reflect the house's relationships with one another. There are three categories of houses that group four together: angular houses, succedent houses, and cadent houses. These categories alternate throughout the zodiac wheel and have distinct relationships. Angular houses are considered the most powerful, with their neighboring succedent houses being less powerful, and their neighbor cadent houses being the least powerful of them all. These house categorizations line up with the modalities of the zodiac, with the cardinal, fixed, and mutable signs being grouped in the same way according to their house counterparts. In this chapter, we will look at how angular, succedent, and cadent houses influence their meaning.

# Angular Houses

Corresponding to the cardinal signs, the angular houses are the first house (Aries), the fourth house (Cancer), the seventh house (Libra), and the tenth house (Capricorn). These are the leading houses, representing some of the most fundamental aspects of life. If you look into the meanings of each of these houses, we can see how they create important tent poles for your life. Astrologers consider these four houses to be the basic needs, the things you must have satisfied in order to live a fulfilled life. The first house deals with your base identity and will form the way that you construct your sense of self. The fourth house, symbolizing home and family, represents the second of the four integral aspects of life. The seventh house comes in with the third foundational quality, which is close, intimate relationships. Finally, the tenth house represents professional ambition and status. All four of these houses are needed to hold up the others, representing the strongest four values.

Because the angular houses are so foundational, those with at least one natal planet in all four of these houses will be incredibly balanced individuals. They will have a firm grip on life and their reality on which they can build a very solid foundation and branch out into more superficial things. Those who lack natal planets in any of these four houses will, by contrast, seem and feel more shallow in their identity and relationships. They might struggle to feel things to their full extent or to build a solid and consistent identity. They might also struggle to form truly rock-solid relationships that will propel them into their best selves.

An important aspect of these house positions is pairing. Each set of four houses has two pairs within it—two houses that have a particularly special relationship with one another. In the case of the angular houses, the pairings are the first house with the seventh and the fourth house with the tenth. These pairings are based on the houses' positions on the wheel, with signs that are positioned opposite one another being the pairs. This concept is fairly similar to the sign polarities, which pair zodiac signs with their opposites. This system shows us how certain aspects of each house contrast with and complement each other.

The first pairing within the angular houses is between the first and seventh houses. We have actually already talked about this pairing a little bit with the comparison between the ascendant and the descendant. The first house represents the beginning of the self journey of the first half of the houses, whereas the seventh house represents the beginning of the self-world journey of the other houses. In other words, they are both leaders in their respective categories. If we were to think about these houses in terms of narrative structures, the first house (and by extension, the first six houses) is man versus self, while the seventh house (and by extension, the last six houses) is man versus society.

The second pairing within the angular houses is between the fourth and tenth houses. These houses represent opposite sides of the spectrum in terms of public versus private life. The family-focused fourth house is as private as you can get, while the status-focused tenth house is as public as you can get. They do, however, share some key similarities. They are both focused on duty and relate to established institutions. They don't deal much with the realms of pleasure or desire but rather the things we owe. Still, they are opposing houses that preside over two very different facets of life.

## Succedent Houses

The succedent houses correspond to the fixed signs and consist of the second house (Taurus), the fifth house (Le0), the eighth house (Scorpio), and the eleventh house (Aquarius). These signs are slightly less foundational than their angular counterparts, but they all still function in most people's lives as important forces. The succedent signs thus take up a slightly less necessary position in the houses. If you are lacking in one or even all of these areas, you can still live a fulfilling life, especially if you have a lot of angular houses. However, having all angular houses and no succedent or cadent houses can make life a little boring without all those other little aspects and twists and turns that make it interesting.

The first pairing that exists within the succedent houses is between the second and eighth houses. The second house represents the material or financial world while the eighth house represents the mysterious, nonmaterial world. You can see how these signs would be opposed, one presiding only over wealth and prosperity and the other presiding over only the higher, spiritual forces that don't consider the earthly world below. They do, however, have a point of connection in the form of upward mobility. Money and spiritual guidance alike both have an infinitely expanding goal that attempts to reach beyond what the person might have been born into. Yet, besides this, these two houses deal with two fairly oppositional parts of life.

The fifth and eleventh houses make up the other duality in the succedent houses. While the fifth house governs over pleasure, the eleventh house governs over friendship. These houses might seem similar on the surface, both dealing somewhat with interpersonal relationships and even love, but that is where the similarities end. At their core, these are very oppositional houses. The fifth house is ultimately an inherently individualistic house. Yes, it can deal with certain relationships in your life but mostly as vehicles for pleasure. There is no duty under the fifth house, nor obligation. If you are a parent, it is because your child brings you joy. In the eleventh house, however, the communities you build come with obligations and duties. You must take care of others under this house in order to be taken care of in turn. So, while they may seem similar, these two signs stand on opposite ends of individualism.

# Cadent Houses

The final category within the house positions is cadent houses, which are based on the mutable signs and contain the third house (Gemini), the sixth house (Virgo), the ninth house (Sagittarius), and the twelfth house (Pisces). The cadent houses are significantly less central than the angular and succedent houses. If you have too many cadent houses, you could get stuck in the world of possibilities or options, never being able to take action. This is why those with too many cadent houses in their chart can come across as flaky and might lack a strong identity or relationships. However, this is not always completely true, since there are some valid reasons you should absolutely have cadent houses in your chart. These are considered the "abstract" houses, the ones where ideas have not yet come to fruition. You need some of these to keep a sense of possibility, variety, and mystery in your life.

The first duality within the cadent houses is between the third and ninth houses. The third house is all about communication, while the ninth house is all about learning. Like the second and eighth houses, they might on the surface seem similar, but they are opposing in a parallel way. The third house is how you present yourself and your ideas to the world, how you best articulate the thoughts in your head. The ninth house, however, is all about how you take in new information, the way you process new things and allow yourself to be shaped by them. In other words, the third house is all about output while the ninth house is all about input.

# Pillar 5:
# Birth Charts

All of the things we have been talking about so far in this book encompass what is called the "birth chart." This is the cumulative representation of all the zodiac, planetary, house, and other astrological principles of your birth. Essentially, the birth chart is an astrological representation of the night sky at the time (and place) of your birth that will tell you all you need to know about your natal astrology. You can find all your planets and their corresponding signs and houses as well as your sun and moon signs in your birth chart. It is the centralized location for all your astrological information. In this pillar, we will show you how to bring together all of the many facets we have discussed throughout this book. You will be able to conglomerate everything you have learned so far in the form of your birth chart. This pillar is separated into two chapters, each with a slightly different focus. The first chapter, 12, will instruct you on how to create a birth chart using information relating to your birth. The next chapter will instruct you on what to do with the sum of information on your birth chart as well as inform you of some extra stray pieces of information we have not covered elsewhere in the book. At the end of this pillar, you will be more knowledgeable about birth charts in general and yours in particular, and you'll be able to cast and interpret many important astrological events.

# Chapter 12:
## Creating Your Birth Chart

B efore you can read your birth chart, you need to create it. Designed to put all your astrological information in one place, astrologers have been creating birth charts for thousands of years. Obviously, given the varying levels of complexity involved in astrology, casting a birth chart can range from extremely easy to very difficult. You can likely do your simpler calculations yourself as an amateur astrologer, but for the more complex calculations, you might need to consult an online calculator or a professional astrologer. In this chapter, we will give you some of the most pertinent information surrounding the calculation of your birth chart.

## Getting Started

Now that you understand the birth chart and all the things that it can encompass, you will need to figure out what yours looks like. But how do you do this? It's not like you can go back in time and chart all the sun, moon, star, and planet positions at the time of your birth. Well, luckily all the planetary bodies involved in your chart move in fairly regular patterns that can be backtracked mathematically. So, no matter when you were born, you will be able to retroactively create a picture of the sky at the time of your birth. Furthermore, astronomers have records of all the planetary positions dating much further back than the birth year of anyone alive today. Whether you research these things yourself or consult the experts, you will be able to get very clear answers on all these positions at your specific date, time, and location of birth. Location is important for time zone purposes. Obviously, the most important thing is that you know your basic information yourself. The basic information you will need to know with absolute certainty is the date, the time (to the hour), and the geographical location of your birth (meaning the town or city). You will not be able to calculate your birth chart to its full accuracy if you do not have all three of these pieces of information. So, before you start casting, you will need to consult with whoever you need to, or even medical records, to ensure that you are completely accurate in your birth information. From there, you can start casting!

## Online and Expert Birth Charts

Before we get into the "how," you should know that you don't necessarily have to cast your birth chart on your own. Many of the determinations you need to make will be complex as you will need to make complicated calculations about the phases of the moon, the positions of the planets, and the planet rotations at the time of your birth. All of these things can be found online but might require more digging. In the case of all aspects of your birth chart, to receive a complete and accurate picture of your astrological sign, you have the option to consult an expert or an online birth chart calculator. In terms of online calculators, there are many free versions as well as some paid versions that have more in-depth descriptions. Some even include long profiles for each of your signs and their relationships with one another. These will provide interpretations for you in addition to your birth chart, so they might be useful if you are not yet as knowledgeable as you would like to be in all of the sign meanings. For interpretive (and casting) purposes, you might also want to consult an astrologer. These people will not only be able to cast for you and give a basic description of your chart, but they will also be there for you to ask questions and possibly provide a more individually tailored profile, depending on the service. If you want the easiest, most accurately calculated version of your birth chart, you have the option to consult one of these things, even just to verify that your calculations were correct.

# Calculating Sun, Moon, and Rising

For those who want to calculate your own birth chart, we will now move on to the instructional aspect. Right off the bat, you will notice that some aspects of your birth chart are easier to calculate than others. These are the things that are on very regular schedules that don't change from year to year. However, there are some things that are more complex and will require you to look at planetary records for the time you were born. In this section, we will look at how to calculate your three foundational signs: the sun, the moon, and the rising.

## Calculating Your Sun

The sun is by far the easiest sign in the zodiac to calculate. You will only need your day of birth on the calendar. Dates for sun zodiac signs never change because our calendar is based around them. So, you can simply consult your date of birth, regardless of the year, and find your sun sign. In Chapter 2, we included the dates of birth associated with all the signs, so you can simply refer back to those when calculating your sun sign. Again, the time of day, year, and location of your birth have no bearing on your sun sign. No matter what is going on with the rest of your chart, everyone born on May 31st will be a Gemini and everyone born on February 10th will be an Aquarius.

## Calculating Your Moon

The moon is more difficult to calculate since you will need the exact date and time, to the hour, of your birth. You will not, however, need your location. The moon's zodiac changes every 2½ days, so you will have to find out what sign your moon was in at the time of your birth. You can usually find this information through records that list the different zodiac signs of the moon. The easiest way is to search your day, month, year, and time of birth online with "moon zodiac" attached. You should be able to come up with your moon sign from this search. You might also be able to find a book of moon records from which you can calculate your moon sign, given that you were born within the book's range. One of these two ways is necessary to calculate your moon.

## Calculating Your Rising

To calculate your rising, you will need to know all of your pertinent birth information, including date, year, time, and location. Your rising sign is fairly easy to calculate thanks to rising charts. Rising charts show the relationship between your sun sign and your rising sign. Even though risings are not as regular as the sun sign, they shift on a regular axis relative to the sun, which means you can use your sun to calculate your rising. The rising chart will show you a simple cross section of sun signs and birth times. For the sake of simplicity, the chart uses standardized time zones, meaning you will have to convert your birth time to the standard time zone. From there, you can simply follow the X-axis showing your sun sign to the Y-axis showing your time of birth to find the square containing your rising sign. So, for example, if you are a Leo and were born between 6 and 8 p.m., then you are a Pisces rising. Consulting one of these charts is the simplest way to calculate your rising. Of course, you can always follow the same instructions as with the moon and simply look up your date and time of birth to find your rising. Either way, you should have an easy time calculating your rising sign.

## Calculating Your Planets

The planets function very similarly to the moon in that there is no regular pattern of how they move relative to our human calendars. Because the sun and the rising sign are tied to the turn or orbit of the earth, they can be calculated by standard means. However, the planets, like the moon, need to be calculated based on orbit records. When finding each of your planets' zodiac signs, you should conduct an internet search similar to finding out your moon sign. Using a search phrase such as "date/time [planet] zodiac" should suffice. Your outer planets will also be easier to calculate since they remain in the same phases for longer periods of time. However, they do sometimes tend to move into a different sign very briefly before snapping back to their original sign. Make sure to keep track of these differences so that you don't miscalculate any outer planets.

## Calculating Your Houses

The houses are actually very easy to calculate simply because you have already done it! Remember that your rising sign is actually just another name for your first house. If you can calculate your rising sign, you will instantly know the rest of your houses. They should proceed in order from your first house. So, if your first house (or rising, or ascendant) is in Leo, then your second house would be in Virgo, your third in Libra, and so forth. However, it is important to note that cusps and angles might affect this clean order of your houses. If you want to ensure that you are calculating all your houses 100% correctly, then you will have to consult an online calculator. This way, you might find out about some angles that could cause two of your houses in a row to be in one sign. Better to be sure than have an inaccurate chart!

## Calculating Retrogrades

When you calculate your planets, your source may or may not tell you whether a planet was in retrograde. Thinking back to our chapter on retrogrades, you will remember that this is a critical aspect of your chart, carrying a completely different meaning than a non-retrograde planet. When you look at your planets, you should check whether it was in retrograde at the time of your birth to ensure that you have the right phase of the planet.

# Chapter 13:
# Reading Birth Charts

Your birth chart will likely look very complicated at first, especially if you don't have a baseline knowledge of general astrology. However, once you understand the role of all the celestial bodies in your birth chart, the complicated markings will start to become clear and you will begin being able to discern important things about your relationships with the stars and planets. In this chapter, we will get into some of the specific ways you should be reading your birth chart.

## What Should I Look For in My Birth Chart?

The specific areas you should be paying attention to in your birth chart are, well, all of them! But it can be hard to know where to start. For the purposes of clarity, you can follow the structure of this book as a general guide to understanding your birth chart. The first things we talked about in this book were the sun, moon, and rising signs. These are the bread and butter of your zodiac profile. They tell you some of the most important basic information about yourself and will give you a clear entry point when constructing your astrological identity. Remember to also consider the different zodiac groupings, like polarities and modalities, to get a more complete sense of your zodiac profile. Then, you can move on to the planets, which will give you deeper insight into how the zodiac signs play out in subtler and more specific aspects of your life. You might not initially connect with your sun sign only to realize that the planets underlying it influence the sun sign and make it more relatable to you. Then, you can move on to the houses, giving your planets and star signs even more clarity and nuance. This methodology will give you a near-complete view of your birth chart as well as your whole astrological identity. There are, however, a few stray things that will matter to your birth chart that we have not yet discussed. In this section, we will look at some of these extra little things that you should keep an eye out for on your birth chart and what they mean for you and your place in astrology.

## House Cusps

Cusps are a very contentious issue in astrology. Many people claim to be born on the "cusp" of two different signs when they really mean that they were just born near the edge of the divide between two signs. When it comes to sun signs, most astrologers will dismiss this idea. They maintain that your sun will be firmly in one sign but concede that you might be a more difficult sun to categorize given your specific birth time or year. So, for example, if you are born at the stroke of midnight on June 20, does that make you a Gemini or a Cancer? Well, it actually depends on the specific year, which you can look up in more detail if you are unsure about your sign. It is guaranteed, however, that you will be firmly one or the other and cannot convincingly argue influence from both signs.

However, when it comes to planets and houses, this is a different story. Because houses are calculated as a matter of degrees, the house that a certain planet falls under is a little messier. Thus, some astrologers agree that being born within a certain small degree of the dividing line between two houses can be considered a cusp and can therefore cause influence from both houses. The jury is still out over the precise degree, but the cusp still stands. So, for example, if you were born when Venus was in the third house but within 10 degrees of the fourth house, then you might have your Venus traits straddling the realms of both communication as well as home and family. Pay close attention to the degrees on the planet-house section of your birth chart as you might be a cusp baby!

## Quadrants

Similar to how all the aspects of astrology have categories, the birth chart has its own categories. These categories are called the quadrants, and they represent the journey of life from birth through youth to maturity. This journey is similar to the Major Arcana of the Tarot, which represents the journey of The Fool through trials culminating with enlightenment, or The World card. Starting with the horizontal radius on the left side, or your ascendant sign, these quadrants move clockwise until they reach the 12th house, just under the ascendant. The first quadrant (comprised of the first three houses) deals with your initial identity and personal foundation. The second quadrant, in the top right section, represents the behavioral patterns that form through-out your youth. This will usually determine your direction in life and your sensibilities regarding politics, values, and relationships. The third quadrant, or bottom right, represents a midlife perspective shift. This shift will come from gaining experience that might be disillusioning, enlightening, or even both. A more realized version of yourself will emerge from this stage. Finally, the fourth house represents maturity and reaping rewards. You should finally be seeing the outcomes of your life and appreciating what you have accumulated, be it wealth, family, fame, happiness, or even just beautiful memories. It is the culmination of the quadrants and the most fulfilled of all.

## Lunar Nodes

Have you ever gone outside to observe a lunar or solar eclipse? Most people have. They are amazing visual feasts. However, did you know that these events are also important in astrology? These moments when the moon and sun overlap in your chart, known as lunar nodes, have a significant role to play in your life's journey. Although you might only be able to see an eclipse once every few years in one particular location, these lineups actually happen at regular intervals. In fact, the nodes go through the signs of the zodiac in perfect order, changing signs roughly every 18 months. Thus, everyone born in that period will have the same lunar nodes, much like the yearly Chinese zodiac. What is especially interesting about lunar nodes is that there will be two on everyone's chart. They are known as the North node and the South node. These two nodes will always be on opposing sides of the zodiac, creating an opposing contrast between one sign and its opposite. Thus, if your North node is in Aquarius, your South node will have to be in Leo, or if your North node is in Taurus, your South node will have to be in Scorpio, and so on. Here, we will look a little deeper into the North and South nodes and what they mean for you and your life's journey.

## North Node

Your North node represents your destiny or the events that will transpire throughout your life that you might not have control over. This is a call to action that will take all the effort inside of you, but it will be worth it. If you feel the need to create great art, climb a mountain, give to others, or any other great life goal, that is your North node talking. No doubt this North node journey will take you far out of your comfort zone, but it will be a journey absolutely worth taking.

## South Node

The South node, on the other hand, represents the abilities and interests innate within you. These might not come with a strong calling, but they will be things that are very easy for you. This innate ability does not always align with your North node calling. In fact, they are often misaligned to create important challenges for you in life. You might find that doing math problems comes as second nature, but it is really writing that calls you to action, even if it is not an innately easy task. Your South node qualities will always be there for you, though, even if you choose not to pursue them in your life journey. These help us build a sense of identity early in life and can give us the earned confidence to pursue what really drives us.

# Reading Combinations

One of the most complex aspects of your chart is how all your signs combine together to form something cohesive. It might be overwhelming to calculate so many different aspects of your chart. You'll probably find that you have almost every sign represented somewhere in your chart, which can be confusing to a beginner astrologer. How do you know what it means to have a Pisces sun, a Taurus moon, and a Scorpio rising? Those signs seem so different from one another, so how can you have all three of them in your chart? If you feel truly lost, you can always go to an astrologer and consult their take on the specific combinations of signs. There have also been many books written that painstakingly describe every single possible combination of the signs. For the sake of time, we will not be listing all these combinations, which would take up multiple books in and of themselves, but we will give you some useful tips on how to read your birth chart combinations.

The first important tip is to start with your sun sign. Learn all there is to know about that sign. Even if you have many other signs in your chart, your sun sign will preside over all of them, so it should always be your starting point. Use it as a springboard for combinations, looking at how all the different signs in your chart work under your sun sign. From there, another important technique is to look for patterns. All your signs add up to form your distinctive personality, so it is useful to note if there are any trends among signs. Look back on some of the early chapters of this book where we talk about sign groupings, such as modalities and elements. You might notice that you have a lot of fire in your chart, which means that your overall personality leans toward the fire element qualities. Similarly, you might notice that you have overwhelmingly negative signs in your chart, which means you lean more toward feminine energy. All these categories can help you start to grasp a sense of your birth chart as a whole and examine how your signs mingle together to create something truly unique to you!

# Conclusion

$A$strology is one of the most mysterious and complicated fields out there, but with the right education, you can start to get a good grasp on how it works. Throughout this book, you have learned some of the most important and foundational concepts in astrology. You have learned about the 12 signs of the zodiac and all their primary and secondary traits. You have also seen how these signs interact with others, grouping them into elements, modalities, and polarities. Next, you were given an introduction to how the planets figure into the zodiac, learning the distinctive differences between how the sun, moon, and each of the planetary bodies interact with the signs. After that, we pivoted to the houses and looked at how this system of dividing the night's sky relates to your life journey and the way you pursue your goals. Finally, we gave you some important tips and advice on how to create and read your birth chart. Through all of these aspects, you have gained a very solid foundation in astrology and are now on your way to becoming an expert!

So, what can you do with this information? How can you employ these astrological principles to better live your life and work toward a good future? The first step is to truly allow your birth chart to wash over you. Read in-depth descriptions of all your planet signs and houses to get a good profile of who you are. Look for patterns like common elements or quadrants in your chart. Allow these signs to interact in order to fill out a distinctive profile of who you are astrologically. Don't worry if you feel like some of your signs don't really describe you very well. This is normal. Sometimes signs exist only within certain contexts or your shadow self. They might also be signs that represent a direction your life will take or a future version of yourself. Truly taking in your astrological chart is the first thing you should do when beginning your astrological journey.

Then, you need to start bringing astrology into your everyday life. When meeting people, consider your signs around relationships and sociability to gain insight into your behavior. Consider signs that are compatible with your own to get a sense of what kind of people you should be trying to attract in your life. When planning your career, look at your lunar nodes to tease out the relationship between your dreams and your abilities. Your chart, if respected and interpreted properly, will be a foundational aspect of your life, showing you who you are in ways you might never have considered. If you take anything away from this book, I hope that it's that you are written in the stars. You have a beautiful connection to the sky above your head and the celestial bodies that guide your life. Astrology is about reaching out to touch them.

# Glossary

**Angular houses:** The strongest houses in the birth chart consisting of houses 1, 4, 7, and 10.

**Aries:** A zodiac sign characterized by ambition and social magnetism; symbolized by the ram.

**Aquarius:** A zodiac sign characterized by uniqueness and social community; symbolized by the water carrier.

**Ascendant house:** Also known as the first house, it is the house just over the horizon.

**Birth chart:** A complete account of your signs, planets, and houses.

**Cadent houses:** The least powerful houses in the chart consisting of houses 3, 6, 9, and 12.

**Cancer:** A zodiac sign characterized by a focus on family and relationships; symbolized by the crab.

**Capricorn:** A zodiac sign characterized by fiscal ambition; symbolized by the goat.

**Cardinal sign:** One of the visionary signs consisting of Aries, Cancer, Libra, and Capricorn.

**Chiron:** A large asteroid in between Jupiter and Saturn that has an influence on astrology.

**Complementary signs:** Signs that are in the same modality but share an important oppositional quality.

**Descendant house:** Also known as the seventh house, it marks the halfway point in the house cycle.

**Fixed sign:** A category of sign that is characterized by hard work consisting of Taurus, Leo, Scorpio, and Aquarius.

**Gemini:** A zodiac sign characterized by social communication; symbolized by the twin.

**House:** A method of dividing the night sky in relation to the horizon consisting of 12 distinct areas.

**House position:** Groups of the houses that correspond to the modalities of the zodiac.

**Inner planets:** The first five planets in the solar system, including the sun and moon but not the earth, consisting of the sun, the moon, Mercury, Venus, and Mars.

**Jupiter:** The fifth planet from the sun; characterized by philosophy.

**Leo:** A zodiac sign characterized by pride and charm; symbolized by the lion.

**Libra:** A zodiac sign characterized by malleability and diplomacy; symbolized by the scales.

**Lunar node:** A moment in your birth chart where the sun and the moon align in a certain sign.

**Mars:** The fourth planet from the sun; characterized by aggression.

**Mercury:** The first planet from the sun; characterized by intellectualism.

**Moon sign:** The sign that the moon is in when you were born; influences your inner self.

**Mutable sign:** A more low-key sign in the zodiac consisting of Gemini, Virgo, Sagittarius, and Pisces.

**Neptune:** The eighth planet from the sun; characterized by the ideal world.

**North node:** One of the lunar nodes on the birth chart representing your life's destiny.

**Outer planets:** The outer five planets from the sun consisting of Jupiter, Saturn, Uranus, Neptune, and Pluto.

**Pisces:** A zodiac sign characterized by emotional availability; symbolized by the fish.

**Pluto:** The ninth planet from the sun; characterized by the relationship between the collective and the ego.

**Polarities:** Dualities within the signs that are characterized by yin and yang energy.

**Quadrant:** A quarter of the birth chart that represents one-quarter of your life's journey.

**Retrograde:** When a planet moves counter to its orbit, from the perspective of earth, thereby reversing the planet's meaning.

**Sagittarius:** A zodiac sign characterized by easygoingness; symbolized by the archer.

**Saturn:** The sixth planet from the sun; characterized by limitation.

**Scorpio:** A zodiac sign characterized by private intensity; symbolized by the scorpion.

**Sign:** The constellation a particular celestial body passes through in the zodiac.

**South node:** One of the lunar nodes representing your innate abilities.

**Succedent houses:** The less intense houses consisting of 2, 5, 8, and 11.

**Sun sign:** The constellation the sun is passing through at the time of your birth.

**Tarot:** A type of card deck with a strong relationship to the zodiac; used for interpretation and prediction purposes.

**Taurus:** A zodiac sign characterized by dependability; symbolized by the bull.

**Uranus:** The seventh planet from the sun; characterized by destruction and renewal.

**Venus:** The second planet from the sun; presides over love and relationships.

**Virgo:** A zodiac sign characterized by strong organization; symbolized by the maiden.

**Yang:** A foundational concept in Chinese philosophy; characterized by positivity, light, and masculine energy.

**Yin:** A foundational concept in Chinese philosophy; characterized by negativity, dark, and feminine energy.

**Zodiac:** The 12 constellations that make up the cycle of astrology.

# References

*Angles and angular houses in astrology.* (n.d.). Molly's Astrology. https://www.mollysastrology.com/topic/angular-houses/

*Aquarius and Leo: Love and friendship compatibility.* (2020, June 19). Thought Catalog. https://thoughtcatalog.com/january-nelson/2020/06/aquarius-leo-compatibility/

*Aries and Libra: Friendship, sex, and love compatibility.* (2021, March 9). Thought Catalog. https://thoughtcatalog.com/january-nelson/2021/03/aries-and-libra/#:~:text=Libra%20and%20Aries%20can%20work

*Beginners corner: Cusps and interceptions.* (n.d.). Big Sky Astrology with April Kent. https://bigskyastrology.com/beginners-corner-cusps-and-interceptions/#:~:text=%E2%80%9CCusps%E2%80%9D%20refer%20to%20the%20division

Bejan Daruwalla, C. (n.d.). *Pisces compatibility with Virgo.* The Times of India. https://timesofindia.indiatimes.com/astrology/zodiacs-astrology/pisces/pisces-compatibility-with-virgo/articleshow/90457951.cms

Brown, M. (n.d.). *If your zodiac sign doesn't feel like a fit, look to your big 3.* Shape. https://www.shape.com/lifestyle/mind-and-body/sun-moon-rising-sign-meaning#:~:text=While%20your%20sun%20sign%20speaks

Campion, N. (2018). *Astrology in Ancient Greek and Roman culture.* In *NASA ADS.* https://ui.adsabs.harvard.edu/abs/2018oeps.book...46C/abstract

Cartwright, M. (2018, May 16). *Yin and Yang.* World History Encyclopedia. https://www.worldhistory.org/Yin_and_Yang/#:~:text=In%20Chinese%20mythology%2C%20Yin%20and

*Cast your horoscope.* (n.d.). Scribd. https://www.scribd.com/document/144923092/Cast-Your-Horoscope

*Chiron | astronomy.* (n.d.). Britannica. https://www.britannica.com/topic/Chiron-astronomy

*Co-Star: Hyper-personalized, real-time horoscopes.* (2020). Costarastrology. https://www.costarastrology.com/natal-chart/

*Development of astrology from ancient to modern times.* (n.d.). Britannica. https://www.britannica.com/summary/astrology

Faragher, A. K. (n.d.). *What each "house" represents in your birth chart.* Allure. https://www.allure.com/story/12-astrology-houses-meaning

*The four quadrants in astrology: Where your main focus in this lifetime.* (n.d.). Cosmic Cuts. https://cosmiccuts.com/en-ca/blogs/healing-stones-blog/quadrants-in-astrology#:~:text=Quadrant%201%20includes%20the%201st

*Here's what it means if you have retrograde planets in your natal chart.* (2020, May 25). Well+Good. https://www.wellandgood.com/retrograde-planets-in-natal-chart/

*Horoscope obsessed? It might be time to read up on Vedic astrology too.* (2020, May 29). Mindbodygreen. https://www.mindbodygreen.com/articles/vedic-astrology-101

*How to create an astrological chart for free.* (n.d.). WikiHow. https://www.wikihow.com/Create-an-Astrological-Chart

*How to find your rising sign (with pictures).* (n.d.). WikiHow. https://www.wikihow.com/Find-Your-Rising-Sign

*How to interpret north nodes & south nodes to find your true purpose.* (2020, December 28). Mindbodygreen. https://www.mindbody-green.com/articles/astrology-101-north-nodes-south-nodes-reveal-your-life-purpose#:~:text=Astrologers%20use%20the%20lunar%20 nodes

*Inner planets in astrology: Planetary meanings and more.* (n.d.). WikiHow. https:// www.wikihow.com/What-Are-the-Inner-Planets-in-Astrology

*Is your zodiac sign cardinal, fixed or mutable?* (n.d.). Bed Threads. https://bedthreads. com.au/blogs/journal/cardinal-fixed-mutable-astrology-signs#:~:text=In%20 astrology%2C%20there%20are%20three

*Learn the purpose of an astrological birth chart, and how to read one.* (n.d.). Live-About. https://www.liveabout.com/learning-to-interpret-birth-charts-207239

Mahtani, N. (n.d.). *Your astrology birth chart reveals more than you might expect.* Nylon. https://www.nylon.com/astrology-birth-chart

*The meaning behind each modality in astrology.* (2021, October 16). Well+Good. https://www.wellandgood.com/modality-astrology/

*Modalities in astrology and their meaning.* (n.d.). Astrology. https://www.astrology. com/modalities

*Modalities: Cardinal.* (n.d.). Astrology. https://www.astrology.com/modalities/ cardinal

*Modalities: Fixed.* (n.d.). Astrology. https://www.astrology.com/modalities/fixed

*Modalities: Mutable.* (n.d.). Astrology. https://www.astrology.com/modalities/ mutable

*Modern astrology.* (n.d.). Astrodienst Astrowiki. https://www.astro.com/astrowiki/ en/Modern_Astrology

Montúfar, N. (2022, April 20). *Everything you need to know about that Taurus moon in your birth chart.* Cosmopolitan. https://www.cosmopolitan.com/lifestyle/ a39777529/taurus-moon-meaning/#:~:text=Your%20Taurus%20Moon%20 exudes%20sensuality

*The need-to-know traits and qualities of every single zodiac sign.* (n.d.). Shape. https:// www.shape.com/lifestyle/mind-and-body/zodiac-signs-meanings-dates

*Neptune and Pluto in the signs.* (n.d.). Cafe Astrology. https://cafeastrology.com/ natal/neptune-pluto-signs.html

*The planets in astrology and their meaning.* (n.d.). Astrology. https://www.astrology. com/planets

*Planets in astrology—Lesson 5.* (n.d.). Astrolibrary. https://astrolibrary.org/planets/

*Retrograde: Planets in retrograde meanings.* (n.d.). Astrology. https://www.astrology. com/retrograde

Robinson, K. (n.d.). *Polarity in astrology: Meaning and opposite signs.* Astrology. https://www.astrology.com/article/what-does-polarity-mean-in-astrology/

Saint Thomas, S. (2020, March 24). *Everything to know about the zodiac signs and their elements.* Allure. https://www.allure.com/story/ zodiac-signs-elements-fire-earth-air-water

*The seven-day week and the meanings of the names of the days.* (n.d.). Crowl. https:// www.crowl.org/Lawrence/time/days.html

Shakespeare, W. *Hamlet.* (c. 1600). https://www.gutenberg.org/files/1524/1524- h/1524-h.htm

Stardust, L. (2022, January 26). *Literally everything you need to know about under-standing nodes in your birth chart.* Cosmopolitan. https://www.cosmopolitan. com/lifestyle/a30198931/north-south-node-meaning-placement-birth-chart/

Thomas, K. (2022, October 3). *Don't freak out, but you probably have some retrograde planets in your birth chart.* Cosmopolitan. https://www.cosmopolitan.com/ lifestyle/a41389256/retrograde-planets-birth-chart/

Trentin, S., & Sneed, D. (2018, June 14). *The Hellenistic period-cultural & historical overview.* Department of Classics. https://www.colorado.edu/clas-sics/2018/06/14/hellenistic-period-cultural-historical-overview#:~:text=The%20 three%20centuries%20of%20Greek

*12 astrological houses—Astrology lesson 4.* (n.d.). Astrolibrary. https://astrolibrary.org/ houses/

Ward, K. (2019, February 26). *Why doing your birth chart will help you figure out your life.* Cosmopolitan. https://www.cosmopolitan.com/uk/entertainment/ a26085821/birth-chart/

*What are the Greek classical elements? (with pictures).* (n.d.). Cultural World. https:// www.culturalworld.org/what-are-the-greek-classical-elements.htm

*What your Chiron sign reveals about your greatest strengths & weaknesses.* (2018, May 9). Mindbodygreen. https://www.mindbodygreen.com/articles/what-your-chiron-sign-says-about-you#:~:text=In%20modern%20astrology%2C%20 Chiron%20represents

*Why a Gemini-Sagittarius relationship proves that opposites attract.* (n.d.). Bustle. https://www.bustle.com/life/gemini-sagittarius-zodiac-sign-compatibility-as-trologers-love#:~:text=Are%20Gemini%20%26%20Sagittarius%20A%20 Good

*Why a Taurus-Scorpio relationship can be a constant struggle.* (n.d.). Bustle. https://www.bustle.com/life/taurus-scorpio-zodiac-sign-compatibility-astrologers-love

*Zodiac signs and their dates.* (2017, July 25). Universe Today. https://www.universetoday.com/38076/zodiac-signs-and-their-dates/

*Zodiac: Symbols, dates, & facts.* (2018). Encyclopædia Britannica. https://www.britannica.com/topic/zodiac

**Image References**

Image 1: OpenClipart-Vectors (2013). https://pixabay.com/vectors/signs-of-the-zodiac-zodiacal-signs-160494/

Image 2 OpenClipart-Vectors (2013). https://pixabay.com/vectors/signs-of-the-zodiac-zodiacal-signs-160494/

Image 3: OpenClipart-Vectors (2013). https://pixabay.com/vectors/signs-of-the-zodiac-zodiacal-signs-160494/

Image 4: OpenClipart-Vectors (2013). https://pixabay.com/vectors/signs-of-the-zodiac-zodiacal-signs-160494/

Image 5: OpenClipart-Vectors (2013). https://pixabay.com/vectors/signs-of-the-zodiac-zodiacal-signs-160494/

Image 6: OpenClipart-Vectors (2013). https://pixabay.com/vectors/signs-of-the-zodiac-zodiacal-signs-160494/

Image 7: OpenClipart-Vectors (2013). https://pixabay.com/vectors/signs-of-the-zodiac-zodiacal-signs-160494/

Image 8: OpenClipart-Vectors (2013). https://pixabay.com/vectors/
signs-of-the-zodiac-zodiacal-signs-160494/

Image 9: OpenClipart-Vectors (2013). https://pixabay.com/vectors/
signs-of-the-zodiac-zodiacal-signs-160494/

Image 10: OpenClipart-Vectors (2013). https://pixabay.com/vectors/
signs-of-the-zodiac-zodiacal-signs-160494/

Image 11: OpenClipart-Vectors (2013). https://pixabay.com/vectors/
signs-of-the-zodiac-zodiacal-signs-160494/

Image 12: OpenClipart-Vectors (2013). https://pixabay.com/vectors/
signs-of-the-zodiac-zodiacal-signs-160494/

Printed in Great Britain
by Amazon

31709817R00086